D0426396

MISSION COLLEGE
LEARNING RESOURCE SERVICES

3 1215 00021 3469

The Real Estate
Agent's and Investor's
Tax Book

The Real Estate Agent's and Investor's Tax Book

ROBERT IRWIN

RICHARD BRICKMAN

McGRAW-HILL BOOK COMPANY
New York   St. Louis   San Francisco   Auckland   Bogotá
Hamburg   Johannesburg   London   Madrid   Mexico
Montreal   New Delhi   Panama   Paris   São Paulo
Singapore   Sydney   Tokyo   Toronto

Library of Congress Cataloging in Publication Data

Irwin, Robert, date
  The real estate agent's and investor's tax book.

  Includes index.
  1. Real property and taxation—United States.
  2. Real estate sales tax—United States.
  I. Brickman, Richard, joint author. II. Title.
  KF6540.I78   343'.73'054   79–18838
  ISBN 0–07–032061–6

Copyright © 1981 by McGraw-Hill, Inc. All rights reserved.
Printed in the United States of America. No part of this
publication may be reproduced, stored in a retrieval system,
or transmitted, in any form or by any means, electronic,
mechanical, photocopying, recording, or otherwise, without
the prior written permission of the publisher.

1234567890   DODO   8987654321

*The editors for this book were William R. Newton and Esther Gelatt,
the designer was Naomi Auerbach, and the production supervisor
was Paul A. Malchow. It was set in Baskerville
by Offset Composition Services.*

Printed and bound by R. R. Donnelley & Sons Company

KF
0540
.I78

Contents

v

For Michael, Alison, Becky, and little David

Preface

The man or woman who doesn't know federal income tax law and who tries to work in real estate today is operating with a severe handicap. Tax law is involved to some degree in every real estate transaction, whether it be the sale of a personal residence or the purchase of a multimillion-dollar commercial center. Without knowing the tax advantages (or disadvantages) involved, one will simply overlook many good deals. Or, what can be worse, one may make deals for clients or investors that are bad from a tax viewpoint.

This is not to say, certainly, that most agents know nothing of real estate tax law. In almost all states brokers and salespeople must possess a certain minimum knowledge in order to pass state licensing tests. But the old maxim "a little knowledge is worse than none at all" may apply here. Incomplete or incorrect knowledge of tax law as it relates to real estate might lead the agent or investor farther astray and into many more difficulties than simply not knowing anything at all.

Nor is this to say that it is the agent's fault if he or she is not well educated in the field of tax law and real estate. The subject can be tricky and difficult. And the books on it that we have seen and the experts we have talked to tend to make the subject even more difficult through their use of complex and often unintelligible language.

That, in fact, is the reason for this book. Over several years we have been asked many, many questions such as these by agents who want a clear and simple explanation:

- How do I handle a tax-free exchange?
- What are the traps a person can fall into in deferring the gain on the sale of a personal residence?
- What is the difference between an installment sale and a deferred-payment sale?
- What are the new rules for syndication?
- Why isn't there a single, concise book that gives easy-to-read answers to the most common income tax questions on real estate? (There is. You are holding it in your hand.)

This book is our answer to all these questions and hundreds of others. It is not written in "legalese." It does not require a degree in jurisprudence or a CPA's license to understand it. It does deal with both the most common and the most complex tax questions in real estate. It is written in language that the typical agent or investor can understand.

This book is for the real estate agent and the real estate investor. It will show them when and how tax considerations enter a transaction. It will provide them with the tax rules for real estate. It will give them step-by-step examples for working through tax-advantageous deals.

This book will not make deals for you. But it will show you how to make tax-smart deals for yourself.

The authors wish to express their sincere appreciation to the following people, who have contributed their energy and patience toward making this a successful book: Shari Beall, Joan Gray, Amy Parsons, Jeane Kirsch, and Marilyn Mosteller.

ROBERT IRWIN and
RICHARD BRICKMAN

Disclaimer

The purpose of this book is to bring to the reader's attention federal income tax law as it relates to real estate. It is sold with the understanding that the authors and publisher of this book are not involved in providing accounting, legal, or other services of a professional nature. This book is not intended to take the place of an attorney or a certified public accountant, nor is it intended to encourage real estate agents to act as attorneys or CPAs for their clients. Readers should seek the aid of an attorney or other competent professional for all legal and tax advice.

All examples in this book are fictional and are for illustrative purposes only. Since they may or may not be applicable to a reader's own tax situation, care should be taken not to apply them to actual real estate transactions or to property without first securing competent professional advice. In addition, tax law is continually evolving. While all tax matters discussed in this book refer to the IRS code in effect as of this writing, check with your own personal tax specialist for changes that may subsequently have occurred.

The Real Estate
Agent's and Investor's
Tax Book

Introduction: Why You Need to Know about Taxes and Real Estate

It is hard to imagine either an agent or an investor who wouldn't want to know the tax consequences of any deal he or she is involved in. The tax angle, in fact, is what makes some deals possible and others impossible.

This book will go into many of both the simple and the complex deals that individuals who are either agents or investors are likely to encounter. For convenience, however, we'll usually address readers as if they were agents. This is not to slight the investor. Rather, it is simply that in most cases we have found it easier to explain transactions and their tax consequences from the viewpoint of a third party or an agent. What the agent knows, however, a wise investor will want to understand as well.

Of course, we can't cover everything. A complete discussion and explanation of all federal tax law related to real estate would probably take dozens of volumes this size. Also, many areas should only be interpreted by a tax attorney or an accountant-CPA who is aware of the specific property and the particular investors. Which leads us to ask: Just how much should the agent (or investor) know and how much should the agent advise the client?

The answer to the first question is easy. The agent (and investor) should know as much as possible. As we noted in the preface, incomplete or incorrect information can be as harmful (perhaps more so) as none at all.

The answer to the second question is more complex. In most states, the agent is empowered solely to bring buyer and seller together. This includes filling out the blanks in a deposit receipt or sales agreement, but it does not include giving legal advice to the client. In fact, agents who are not also attorneys are cautioned against giving *any* legal advice.

1

Nonetheless, in actual practice it is most often the agent who puts the deal together. And since real estate transactions frequently have significant tax consequences for the principal parties, how the agent puts those deals together can seriously affect the buyers and sellers for good—or for bad.

For example, recently we heard of a broker who arranged a trade between two parties. One party disposed of a house, the other of a four-unit building. The agent made sure that the equities of each party were balanced, arranged for the financing, and concluded the sale. At the time, it seemed like a well-made deal. It was only later that the agent learned, via an angry phone call, that one of the parties had incurred an unexpected and heavy tax liability on the transaction. That trader, needless to say, was furious.

"Why didn't you point out *before* I signed that I would have to pay so much tax!" yelled the angry trader.

The agent was at a loss. He had thought that since there was a simple exchange of equities, no tax liability would occur. When an accountant explained to him that the trader's *basis* in the property in relation to *price, boot,* and many other items also figured into a recognized gain calculation, he was surprised and flustered. He didn't know and he still didn't understand (see the explanation in Chapter 9).

In this case, the agent was able to placate the angry trader by offsetting some of the unexpected tax liability out of his own commission. Needless to say, our agent was chagrined, unhappy, and determined to learn more about taxes.

If the agent arranges for transactions, it is inevitable that he or she will need to know about tax law in order to avoid harming the clients. Again, we repeat, this does not mean giving the clients legal or tax advice. (It may mean, however, knowing when to send the client to an attorney or CPA for such advice.)

Of course, some agents spend their entire careers in real estate without ever handling an exchange. They specialize in the biggest real estate market—houses. Many agents feel that these deals are so simple, from a tax viewpoint, that there is no need to consider helping clients with the tax ramifications of the deals.

Again, this is not the case, and two deals come to mind—one in Los Angeles and the other in Minneapolis. In Los Angeles, a broker we met was selling a home for a couple who had recently sold two other homes, both principal residences. They had sold a principal residence 16 months earlier and had bought another and sold it just 10 months earlier. (Neither husband nor wife had changed employment location.) This was to be their *third* move. They told the agent they had deferred all the gain on the sale of their last two homes under IRS rules. Now they could either sell their present house or rent it out. But since they had done so well deferring gains in the past sales, they planned to sell again. The agent thought it was a good idea, took the listing, and quickly sold the house. The couple felt they would have no immediate taxes to pay because of the sale.

You can imagine the agent's embarrassment and concern when she later learned that because of special provisions in the deferral rule, the deferral of gain which the couple had taken on their *second* house was totally disallowed by the IRS because of the untimely sale of their *third* house. By choosing to sell their third house when they did instead of waiting only a short time longer, they dramatically increased their tax liability. When they called the agent to ask why she hadn't informed them of the tax consequences of the sale, she was able to say only, "I'm sorry."

Another agent in Minneapolis was made just as unhappy by a different sort of circumstance. He was approached by a naval career officer who asked him to sell his principal residence. The naval officer was on temporary leave from Japan, where he had been stationed for the previous 3 years. He wanted our agent to sell his Minneapolis house, which had been rented out for 3 years. He told the agent the only reason he was selling the property was that he planned to defer all his gain under the same rule as the people in our last example.

Our agent was very conscientious. He said he would be glad to take the listing. However, he said that in order to take the deferral benefits (not pay taxes immediately) our naval officer would need to demonstrate that the home truly was his principal residence. He undoubtedly could not do this, since he had been out of the country, living in Japan, for 3 years and had rented out the Minneapolis home for the entire time. The officer would have to reestablish the home as a principal residence by living there again. Once this was done, he could get the deferral benefits and our agent would gladly take the listing.

The officer answered that this was not possible, since he was leaving that very day for Japan and probably wouldn't return for another year.

The agent thought nothing of the conversation until a few weeks later, when he passed by the officer's home. Not only did he see a For Sale sign, but tacked to the For Sale sign was a big "Sold!"

Out of curiosity, the agent called the listing office and talked to the lister. He asked her if she knew that the seller wanted to defer gain yet had not reestablished the home as his principal residence. The lister said she was well aware of the seller's intent but that—according to tax law and the circumstances — it was not necessary to reestablish the property as his residence. He had never lost that status. (See Chapter 1 to see why.) Then she referred our agent friend to a good tax lawyer.

Our agent mused for a very long time about the listing he had let slip through his fingers because of incomplete knowledge.

For the last time we repeat: The agent who is not also an attorney should not give tax or legal advice to a client. But the agent who does not possess accurate tax law knowledge can harm either himself, his client, or both.

1

Selling a Residence: When the Taxable Gain Can Be Deferred—and When It Can't

Day in and day out, sellers across the country ask their agents to clarify how they may defer paying taxes on their gain at the time they sell their principal residence. Almost every seller has heard of the rule, but hardly any seller knows or understands it fully.

Because deferral is such a common question, most agents have a set of standard answers to give, ones that they learned early in their real estate careers. In fact, a typical comment of agents is, "Deferring gain on sale of residence is one of the easiest things a prospect can ask, easy to understand and simple to explain."

Perhaps, but when agents were asked in seminars to explain the tax law on this question, more than seven out of ten were totally wrong! They had been giving their clients erroneous information, and their clients, in turn, had been acting on it.

This is not, of course, to say that there was anything wrong with the agents. It was simply that this material had never been clearly explained to them. In fact, many otherwise exemplary books on real estate spend only a paragraph or two on the subject.

This is also not to say that *deferral or nonrecognition of gain on sale of a principal residence* is difficult or hard to understand. It is quite easy, and therein lies the rub. It looks so easy that it's even easier to make a mistake.

There are many rules which have to be followed under the nonrecognition of gain, and an agent would not be wise simply to assure a client that, for example, he or she will qualify for deferral if a new house is bought within 18 months of the sale of the old one. Suppose the client asks, "Do I have to invest all or some of my gain in the new house?" or, "I sold under an installment contract—how does the rule work for me here?" or, "This is my second sale of principal residence in the last year. Does that create a problem?" or, "I'm over 55. Are there special provisions for me?" or even, "Do I *ever* have to pay the taxes?" or a hundred other questions, some considerably more difficult.

As we've noted earlier, it is the exceptional agent who can readily answer all these exceedingly common questions. To help you become an expert as that exceptional agent, we've divided the nonrecognition rule into 20 parts to allow a quick assimilation of its most essential elements.

1. The taxpayer must purchase a new principal residence within 18 months before or 18 months after the sale of the old residence. In the case of new construction, the taxpayer must begin construction within 18 months and must occupy the new principal residence within 24 months after the sale of the old one.

Winston sold his home and realized a gain on the sale. If he now buys a new principal residence, he can defer the gain, provided the purchase is made within 18 months after the sale of the old residence (or 18 months before it) and provided the other conditions of the rule are met. The purchase of the new principal residence can be made at any time during this total of 36 months. He can rent an apartment for 17 months and 3 weeks, for example, after the sale of the old residence and *take possession* of a new residence on the last day of the eighteenth month and still come under the rule. Figure 1-1 shows the time periods involved.

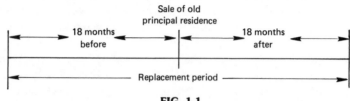

FIG. 1-1

In the case of new construction, the time allowed is increased. The rule of 18 months before sale still applies, however. Now if Winston decides not to buy an existing house but rather to build a new one himself, he must *start construction no later than 18 months after the sale of the old residence and occupy the new residence no later than 24 months after that sale.* The time allowed for new construction is shown in Figure 1-2.

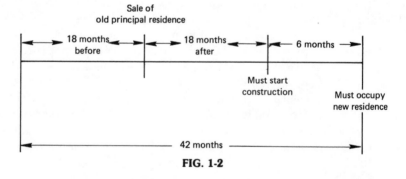

FIG. 1-2

The rule about moving into the newly constructed residence no more than 24 months after the sale of the old one tends to be inflexible. We recently ran into the case of an individual who had not quite completed his home by the 2-year time limit. To try to qualify for the deferral of gain on the sale of his old residence, he moved several pieces of furniture (a bed, dresser, sofa, and dining table) into the not-quite-completed new home and claimed it as his new principal residence. The Internal Revenue Service decided that since he had not actually begun living in the new home, it was not his principal residence, and his claim was disallowed.

Additionally, in general new construction should be *initiated* by the taxpayer. It is not sufficient to simply buy a new house constructed independently by a builder.

2. Both the property sold and the property bought must be the taxpayer's *principal* residence.

Winston considered himself a big-time investor in real estate. In addition to the home in which he lived, he had bought for $25,000 a second home, which he used as a rental property. After 5 years of ownership, he saw the chance to make a healthy profit on his investment. He sold his rental for $50,000 and immediately bought a new rental. He figured his $25,000 gain was free and clear of taxes because it came under the nonrecognition rule.

Winston was way off base. The rule applies only when an individual sells his or her own *principal* residence and buys a new *principal* residence (a taxpayer can have only one principal residence at a time). If either the property being bought or the property being sold is something other than the principal residence (in this case, an investment), the rule *cannot* be applied. Winston had to pay the capital gains tax (see Chapter 7 for how to figure this on the gain). The fact that the property being bought or sold is residential does not in itself make any difference; it must be the *principal* residence.

When selling		*When buying*	
YES	Principal residence	YES	Principal residence
NO	Investment apartment building	NO	Second house
	Investment duplex		Investment duplex
	Second house		Investment apartment building

3. There are clearly defined limits to what qualifies as a principal residence.

Winston's cousin Isabel sold her house and moved into a mobile home. She was still entitled to claim the nonrecognition-of-gain benefit. *A principal residence need not be a house*; it can also be one unit of a duplex, apartment building, or larger residential building. In this case only the part occupied can be claimed, not the whole building. The principal residence can also be a houseboat, a house trailer, a mobile home, or even stock held by a tenant-stockholder in a cooperative housing corporation.

4. All of the gain must be deferred[1] if the new principal residence costs more than the old one, but the new residence need not cost more than the old for *part* of the gain to be deferred.

Our friend Winston finally went ahead and sold his old house for $65,000 and bought a new one for $70,000. Exhibit 1-1 shows how a workup for tax purposes on the sale and purchase looked.

EXHIBIT 1-1

The gain was computed in this fashion:

Selling price of *old* residence		$65,000
Less commission and expenses		−5,000
Adjusted sale price of old residence		$60,000
Cost of *old* residence	$35,000	
Plus improvements	5,000	
Basis of *old* residence		−40,000
GAIN		$20,000

The realized gain on the sale was $20,000. But it was deferred because:

Adjusted sale price of *old* residence	$60,000
Less cost of *new* residence	−70,000
TAXABLE GAIN (new cost more than old)	$ 0

Since the cost of the new residence was higher than the adjusted sale price of the old one, all the $20,000 gain was *not recognized*. Since it was not recognized, he did not immediately pay any federal income taxes on it.

But let's say for a moment that Winston's new house cost only $50,000. Now it's a different story. The sale price, adjusted sale price, and gain realized remain the same as in our first example; but now the cost of the new residence is less than the cost of the old residence:

Adjusted sale price of *old* residence	$60,000
Cost of *new* residence	−50,000
Gain recognized	$10,000

Winston would have to pay taxes on this $10,000 recognized gain, but since his total gain was $20,000, he would not immediately have to pay

[1] The rule is mandatory, not optional.

taxes on the other $10,000. Remember, the rule is that *in order for the entire gain to be deferred, the cost of the new residence must be higher than the adjusted sales price of the old residence. However, if the cost of the new residence is less than the adjusted sale price, part of the gain may still be deferred.* In this case, Winston did not have to pay taxes on 50 percent of his gain. (The amount, of course, will vary according to how much higher the adjusted sales price is than the cost of the new residence.)

5. The taxpayer *need not invest any of the equity* from the old principal residence in the new in order to qualify.

Winston owed about $30,000 on his old principal residence, so that when he sold he netted about $30,000 in cash after expenses. He was planning to put 10 percent down into his new home and put the rest in the bank. Ten percent of the $70,000 cost of the new home is $7,000; this would leave $23,000 in cash for him to dispose of as he wished. But he didn't have to put $7,000 down for tax purposes. If, for example, he was able to get a 100 percent loan on his property — perhaps a Veterans Administration (VA) loan — and put nothing down, he could still take advantage of the nonrecognition rule. He could take the entire $30,000 he received from the sale of his old residence and put it in the bank, or buy four or five new cars, or take an extended world cruise. It makes no difference what you do with the money that is deferred under the nonrecognition rule; none has to be reinvested so long as a new residence is purchased.

6. The taxpayer may eventually have to pay tax on *all* the gain that is deferred.

It is important to understand the difference between the words "defer" and "exclude" as they are used for tax purposes. "Defer" means only to put off until a *later date*. "Exclude" means not to have to pay at all. The tax on the gain under the nonrecognition rule is only *deferred*. It is not excluded. In theory, some day Winston might sell his principal residence and move into a rented apartment. Since the replacement periods will have elapsed, he will owe the tax on the gain ($20,000) from his sale.

But what if Winston sells his principal residence and then buys another? And then sells that and buys yet a third and a fourth, and so on?

The gain he made on the first sale will be *added* onto the gain he makes on the second sale, and so forth, until his last sale of a principal residence, when tax will have to be paid on all the gains! This can add up to a considerable amount of money. Let's take an example, Exhibit 1-2, and see how it works.

EXHIBIT 1-2

First house	Adjusted sale price (price less expenses of sale)	$ 60,000
	Adjusted basis (cost plus improvements)	− 40,000
	GAIN	$ 20,000

Second house	Cost	$ 70,000
	Less gain deferred on first house	− 20,000
	Adjusted basis	$ 50,000

(For the remainder of this example, it will be assumed no improvements were made on the properties.)

	Adjusted sale price	$100,000
	Less adjusted basis	− 50,000
	GAIN	$ 50,000

Third house	Cost	$115,000
	Less deferred gain	− 50,000
	New adjusted basis	$ 65,000
	Adjusted *sale* price	$150,000
	Less adjusted basis	− 65,000
	GAIN	$ 85,000

Fourth house	Cost	$160,000
	Less deferred gain	− 85,000
	New adjusted basis	$ 75,000
	Adjusted *sale* price	$185,000
	Less adjusted basis	− 75,000
	GAIN	$110,000

If the fourth house is his last owned principal residence, Winston will owe taxes on $110,000 of gain upon sale (and expiration of replacement periods for deferral).

This is one of the great perils of the nonrecognition rule — the tax is only *deferred*; it must be paid someday. But, then, what if Winston never goes from an owned house into a rented apartment? What if he lives in the fourth residence until he dies? No income tax will be paid upon his death. Instead, federal estate tax law will come into play and a whole new set of tax rules and basis rules will apply.[2]

What is particularly noteworthy here is that unless Winston reinvests his *equity* each time, when he sells his last house he may not get enough money to pay his taxes. It is often the case that homeowners will put back only a part of their equity. While this may work perfectly well as long as they continue to live in an owned principal residence, when they finally cash in, the practice can catch up with them. For example, if Winston puts only 20 percent ($32,000) down when he purchases his

[2] Federal Tax Reform Act of 1976.

last residence for $160,000 and makes a profit of $25,000 (sale price less cost) when he sells it, he will be netting $57,000, or roughly *half* his taxable gain.

7. If you own a building of which you live in part and rent out part, you can claim benefits only on the part in which you live.

The amount you can claim is in direct proportion to the part in which you live. For example, if you own a triplex (three units), live in one unit, and rent two out, you can claim one-third of the gain from the sale under this rule. But in most circumstances you will have to pay tax in the year of sale on two-thirds of the gain.

8. Even if the taxpayer rents out a principal residence, he or she may still be able to claim benefits under the non-recognition rule.

Renting out your principal residence does not in itself preclude your using the nonrecognition benefits. The United States Tax Court rendered a decision on January 30, 1975, in the case of *Robert G. Clapham*[3] that bears directly on this point. In that case, the taxpayers vacated their old residence in August 1966, moved to another city, and rented a house there until September 1968. From August 1966, they intermittently rented and attempted to sell the old residence until June 1969, when they finally found a purchaser. Although they had not occupied their old residence for nearly 3 years, the time between their purchase of a new residence, September 1968, and the sale of their old one, June 1969, was only 9 months, well within the time provisions of the nonrecognition rule.

The Internal Revenue Service contended that in vacating the old residence with no intention of returning, the taxpayers abandoned it as their principal residence. But the court held for the taxpayers. It said that each case must be decided on the facts and circumstances surrounding it. In the *Clapham* case, rental of their old residence for a temporary period was necessitated by the state of the real estate market (they couldn't sell it at the time), was ancillary to sale efforts, and arose from the taxpayers' use of their old residence as their principal residence.

Merely renting out an old principal residence, therefore, *does not* preclude a seller from using the rule. But remember, the reason it is rented is all-important. If it is rented out simply for investment purposes,

[3] *Robert G. Clapham*, 63 T.C. 505 (1974).

it becomes a piece of investment property and does not qualify as discussed above. If it is rented out because it cannot be sold in the current market, it may qualify.

It is important to understand, however, that the government can be very strict when it comes to deciding what is "abandoning" a principal residence and what is not. In another case, the court held that property was abandoned, because the owner had put all furniture in storage, intending never to live there again, and had rented an apartment for 2 years prior to sale. Also, the house purchased was not considered a principal residence, because for more than a year after the sale of the old residence, the taxpayer continued to live in the apartment and used the new residence only on weekends and holidays. In the case of *William C. Stolk,*[4] the house was not a principal residence, since for 2 years prior to its sale it had been occupied by Stolk's mother while he lived in rented property.

9. There are special exceptions for foreign employment and military service.

The courts have held that if property has been rented out in order to care for it during a period of foreign employment and the owner intends to return, it can still be claimed as a principal residence. In an important case before the tax court, a person in the above circumstances was prevented from obtaining possession on his return to the United States because of rent control regulations. He subsequently sold the house. The court decided to allow his nonrecognition claim, but the Internal Revenue Service has indicated that it will only consider other cases that are factually similar.

The rules are more liberal when it comes to military service. If you are in the United States military services on extended active duty (more than 90 days or for an indefinite period), the replacement times are extended to 4 years. They are totally suspended while you are in a combat zone.

Further, if during this time you rent out your house, you will not be disqualified. One army officer was allowed to claim the nonrecognition rule after he had leased his home to others for 5 years prior to the sale and had claimed *depreciation* on it during this period! The court's decision was prompted because his military duties required him and his family to live in government quarters. (*Arthur R. Barry,* 1971.[5])

---

[4] *William C. Stolk,* 40 T.C. 345 (1963) *aff'd* (2d Cir. 1964), 326 F.2d 760.
[5] *Arthur R. Barry,* 71,179 P-H Memo T.C.

10. Only *one* sale and purchase of a residence is allowed every 18 months. Only the *last* residence purchased during the period is counted.

Our friend Winston was so thrilled by the fact that he didn't have to pay taxes on any gain when he sold his house on Cherry Street for $60,000 and bought a new one on Lemon Court for $70,000 that he figured he'd do it again, particularly since the market was so "hot."

Within a few months, he sold his new residence on Lemon Court for $80,000 and bought yet another residence on Peach Road for $90,000. Since each piece of property he bought cost more than the one he had sold and since each was his principal residence, he figured that he didn't have to worry about taxes but could defer them all under the nonrecognition rule. He was wrong!

For tax deferral purposes, you are allowed only one sale of principal residence *every 18 months*, beginning at the time of the first sale. Since 18 months had not elapsed between the time of the first sale and the last purchase, the government figured Winston's gain as shown in Exhibit 1-3.

EXHIBIT 1-3

Adjusted sale price of first residence	$60,000
Less cost of third residence (last purchased)	−90,000
Since last principal residence cost more than old	$ 0
Adjusted sales price of second residence	$80,000
Cost of second residence on Lemon St. (basis)	−70,000
GAIN (all taxable)	$10,000

Winston had to pay taxes on $10,000, and since the purchase and sale had not been over a period of one year or longer, he had to report this as ordinary income; he could not even claim capital gains benefits! (See Chapter 7 for a full explanation of capital gains.)

If only he'd remembered that you get only one sale every 18 months under the nonrecognition rule and that if more than one sale and purchase occurs, only the last is considered under this rule!

THERE IS ONE EXCEPTION TO THE RULE OF ONE "ROLLOVER" EVERY 18 MONTHS

The Tax Revenue Act of 1978 provides for an exception to the rule we've just discussed. If the taxpayer should move because of a change in employment, then more than one "rollover" every 18 months is allowed. In general the new rule provides that the taxpayer must be moving with a reasonable expectation of being employed at the new location for a substantial period of time. The law is tied to the taxpayer's being entitled to deduct moving expenses.

In general if both geographic and employment duration requirements connected with job relocation are met, so that the taxpayer is entitled to deduct moving expenses, then the rollover benefits are allowed more than once in 18 months. The rules for deduction of moving expenses are complex, and some interpretation is required on the part of the person making them. Consequently, if benefits of the rollover provision are sought because of an employment relocation, a tax attorney or accountant should be consulted.

Tests for determining whether moving expenses may be deducted (and benefits under the new rollover provision allowed) may be:

1. The new place of employment must be at least *35 miles* farther from the old home than the old place of employment was from the old home.

2. The taxpayer must be employed on a full-time basis for at least *39 weeks* out of the 12 months following the move at the new place of employment or in its general vicinity. The second condition may be waived for several reasons including: discharge from employment (unless for willful misconduct); death or disability of the taxpayer; and transfer by an employer (provided the taxpayer can show a reasonable expectation that no transfer was anticipated during the qualifying time period).

See also item 18 in this chapter for an additional discussion.

11. You may increase the "cost" of the new residence after the purchase has been completed.

Winston's Uncle Charley recently had this problem. He sold a home for $70,000 (adjusted sale price) and bought a new one for $60,000. Under the nonrecognition rule, he'd have to pay taxes on $10,000 of the gain on the sale of the old property. But Uncle Charley was enterprising and inventive. He knew he would eventually add a swimming pool, and so he went to the sellers and asked them if, before the sale was completed, they would put in the pool. Of course, he would pay for it, and this would raise the price of the property at least another $10,000. This would put the cost of the new principal residence above the sales price of the old, and he could defer *all* the gain on the sale of his old principal residence.

The sellers, understandably, were not thrilled about doing this. It would mean they would have to wait until the pool was built before they could get their money. Charley "sweetened the pot" by agreeing to pay their mortgage payments during the period the pool was being built and while they still occupied the house! He also agreed to prorate taxes as of the date pool construction *started.*

The pool was dug, the sale made for a price higher than the one at which he had sold his old house, and Uncle Charley was able to defer all his gain. He was out only the mortgage payments and the taxes during the construction period and the headache of arguing with the sellers.

Poor Uncle Charley. If he'd only realized that all this was unnecessary! Remember, a taxpayer has *18 months after the sale of the old residence, or up to 24 months with new construction, to replace it with a new principal residence.* If Charley had simply made the purchase at $60,000 and then added the pool on his own time while he lived on the property, he could have saved all the fuss and trouble. He had the full 18 months (24 with new construction) during which to replace his principal residence. If he had bought at month 12 and added the pool by month 17, he would still have been well within the time limit. He would simply have added the price of the pool to his cost of new residence, coming up with a new adjusted basis for his *new residence.* As long as this was above the $70,000 adjusted *sale* price of his *old* residence, all the tax on gain from the sale of the old residence could be deferred.

12. The cost you incur in fixing up your old house for sale can be deducted, within certain set limits.

Winston kept his house so well maintained that when he sold he didn't have any expenses in fixing it. But if he had not been so neat and had in fact incurred $1,000 in expenses, he could have handled it as shown in Exhibit 1-4.

EXHIBIT 1-4

Selling price	$65,000
Less commission and closing costs	− 5,000
Adjusted sales price	$60,000
Less basis (original cost plus cost of improvements)	−40,000
GAIN REALIZED	$20,000
Now, he could have deducted his fixing-up expenses:	
Adjusted sales price	$60,000
Less fixing-up expenses	− 1,000
NEW ADJUSTED SALE PRICE	$59,000

It is important that the calculations be figured in this way, for, while the fixing-up expenses are deductible when figuring the amount to be deferred under the *nonrecognition* rule, they *cannot be used* when figuring a *recognized* gain.

Also, the rules for fixing up require that the *work be started no more than 90 days before a sales contract is signed and be paid for no more than 30 days after a sale has been completed.* (Note that this can be for more than 120 days, since the escrow period normally occurs between signing the sales contract and recording the deed.) And finally, the work must be for repairing existing property. It cannot be for additions. Fixing a broken window would count; adding a new room would not (but it would increase cost basis).

13. Upon reaching the age of 55, the taxpayer may exclude up to $100,000 of the gain from the sale of a principal residence, but only once in a lifetime.

This rule, added to the tax laws in 1978, applies to sales after July 26, 1978, by persons 55 or over. If the taxpayer is married and filing a separate return, the limit is $50,000.

To qualify for this exclusion, in general, the taxpayer must have used the property as a principal residence for a minimum of three years in the five-year period immediately preceding the date of sale. A special provision in this rule allows any taxpayer who sells a residence before July 26, 1981, and who is 65 by the time of the sale, to have occupied the property for five of the previous eight years (instead of using the above-mentioned three-out-of-five rule). This special provision relates to a former tax rule—so check with your attorney for clarification in your particular case.

The "once-in-a-lifetime" provision is to be strictly interpreted in this rule. If a taxpayer upon reaching the age of 55 elects to take this exclusion and does not have the full $100,000 limit in gain, the difference between the amount claimed and the limit may be lost. For example, if a taxpayer at age 55 only has $55,000 in gain from the sale of a principal residence and elects to take his exclusion, he or she may not later take an additional $45,000 ($100,000 maximum less $55,000 taken). The exclusion may be taken only once in a lifetime regardless of the amount.

The once-in-a-lifetime rule also applies when gain from the sale of a previous residence has been deferred under the nonrecognition rule, provided, of course, there is a sale of the last principal residence.

While this relatively new rule seems quite simple on the surface, its application in specific cases can be quite complicated, necessitating the assistance of a personal tax counselor. There are many peculiarities to the rule. For example, while a single individual who qualifies under the rule may take up to the full $100,000 of exclusion, a married couple who qualify are also limited to only $100,000. The individual who happens to be single has the same exclusion as two individuals who happen to be married.

This has some interesting ramifications. A taxpayer who is married at the time of sale, must have his or her spouse join in the election to use the ruling *even if the property happens to be separate property not held in the spouse's name.* For example, if Helen owns a property separately from her husband, George, he must join with her in any election to take the up to $100,000 exclusion (in the rule) on her property, even though, since it is her own property, he may not share in any of the benefits. Further, if George and Helen should divorce and George later remarry and purchase another piece of property with his new wife, after fulfilling the time requirements, George and his new wife would be prohibited from claiming the up to $100,000 exclusion even though the new wife never had claimed it herself and George had never received any benefits from the election filed when he was still married to Helen. (If he was lucky, George might get together with Helen to revoke the election they had earlier made together. If this were done, then George and his new wife could take it on their new property. George and Helen would have three years after the election was filed to do this. Helen, however, would then be responsible for the taxes on the money originally excluded and for this reason might not be too anxious to go along with George's request.)

Finally, both the up to $100,000 exclusion and the rollover (deferral of gain) *may be used in the same sale.*

14. If your residence is condemned, it is the same for tax deferral purposes as it would be if you had sold it.

If your personal residence is condemned and you are forced to sell, you still come under the provisions of the nonrecognition rule, and you can defer the gain *if you choose to do so.* A separate statement for this purpose, however, must be filed with your tax returns for the taxable year in which your residence was condemned, and you cannot later revoke this election to defer again.

15. Divorcees can each claim one-half the benefits of their combined interest in the residence.

If Winston and his wife, Jennifer, were to divorce and sell their home for what they paid, $70,000 with a deferred gain from a previous home of $20,000, they would now each have a new adjusted sale price of $35,000 with a basis of $25,000. They would split both the selling price and the deferred gain.

16. Gain on sale of principal residence can be deferred even though the sale is made on an installment-contract basis.

Occasionally, a principal residence will not be sold on a cash basis (such as we've been discussing) but on an installment contract. This is increasingly true today, since the skyrocketing price of homes has given owners very large equities. The tax laws have a special rule, as most agents know, that deals with installment sales: If the purchase is to be made in two or more payments and the payment in the first year does not exceed 30 percent of the sale price, then the gain may be reported proportionately as the payments are received.[6]

Natalie, Winston's sister, bought her first house and principal residence for $25,000. Property values jumped in her neighborhood, and 3 years later she sold for $75,000. The buyer gave her $15,000 in cash and a mortgage calling for payments over the next 20 years.

Adjusted sale price	$75,000
Accounted for as follows:	
Cash down (first installment)	$15,000
Mortgage	+60,000
	$75,000

The gain on the sale must be accounted for, and since it was an installment sale, with no more than 30 percent received in the first year (actually only 20 percent was received), it was handled in this manner:

Adjusted sale price	$75,000
Less adjusted basis	25,000

$$\frac{\text{GAIN}}{\text{SALE PRICE}} = \frac{\$50,000}{\$75,000} = \frac{2}{3}$$

The ratio of gain to the total amount of installments is 2:3. That means that two-thirds of each payment is considered gain on which taxes are paid.

The advantage of reporting gain in installments is that when it is spread out over several years, a lower rate might be used in computing the tax (depending, of course, on other income) than if the gain is all reported in one year.

Natalie bought a new principal residence just 6 months after the sale of her old one. Had she bought for higher than the old price, all of her gain could be deferred under the nonrecognition rule. But she bought

[6] See Chapter 15 for details.

a home for only $45,000. This meant that $30,000 of the gain would be recognized while the remainder would be deferred.

Deferred gain	$20,000
Recognized gain	+30,000
Total gain	$50,000

This changed the ratio of gain taxed in each installment of the home considerably. It looked like this:

$$\frac{\text{Gain}}{\text{Sale price}} \quad \frac{\$30,000}{\$75,000} = \frac{2}{5}$$

Now the ratio was 2:5. That meant that two-fifths of each annual payment had to be reported as gain in the year received.

17. When the gain to be deferred is calculated, reduction in gain may be undesirable if the reason for sale has to do with moving from one job to another.

There is a special provision in the tax law that allows certain moving expenses to be deducted from an individual's personal income (Section 217 of the IRS Code). Under the heading of indirect expenses are those involved with the sale of a residence; they include commissions and those closing costs we will note as being allowable at the end of Chapter 2. In general, there are two major limitations (for more specific limitations, a taxpayer should check the Internal Revenue Code or consult an attorney), and these involve amount and distance. The new job must be at least 35 miles farther from the old home than the old job was from the old home, and the amount cannot be more than $3,000.

The catch is that to prevent a double benefit, the IRS does not allow the expenses to be deducted both from personal income and from the sale price when gain is figured. Each taxpayer has to decide which way of figuring will give him or her the greatest advantage. But if the decision should be that the best way is to deduct the amount from personal income, special care must be taken in figuring the gain on sale.

For example, Winston had a friend, Harry, who sold his principal residence after living there for 5 years, for $60,000. He had $5,000 of expenses. Normally, these would be deducted in figuring the adjusted sale price.

Price	$60,000
Less expenses of sale including commission	− 5,000
Adjusted sale price	$55,000

Harry, however, needed as many deductions as he could get on his income taxes that year. It turned out he had sold his principal residence to move to a new job in Los Angeles (he had lived in Minneapolis) and so up to $3,000 of his selling expenses could be used for this purpose. Now the calculation for adjusted sales price looked like this:

Price	$60,000
Expenses remaining after $3,000 was subtracted for use in figuring personal income tax deductions	− 2,000
Adjusted sale price	$58,000

For Harry, the best thing was *not* to deduct the full commission and other expenses from the sale price of his old principal residence when figuring gain. Agents, therefore, should be cautious, when explaining the deferral rule, about assuring clients who are moving from job to job that deducting all selling expenses from the sales price is best for them.

Of course, Harry's maneuver could backfire. The $3,000 difference could create additional capital gain. If Harry bought a new principal residence with a cost of $55,000, he could defer taxes on all of his gain under the first calculation; he would need to pay capital gains tax on a gain of $3,000 under the second.

18. When a taxpayer intends to replace an old principal residence with a new one under the nonrecognition rule, the IRS must be notified in the year of the sale of the old residence, whether or not a new one has already been purchased.

When a replacement of a principal residence takes place within a tax year, the computation for IRS purposes is fairly simple and is handled on Form 2119. Most agents will not be in the position of filling out tax forms for their clients. Nonetheless, a buyer or seller may ask a question or two about the procedure, and the wise agent should at least be familiar with the form. As a convenience, therefore, a copy of Form 2119 is shown in Figure 1-3 (front and back). (It is to be handled by an attorney or CPA.)

As with most IRS forms, the taxpayer is required to fill in the blank spaces on a specially prepared page (Form 2119). If, however, the taxpayer intends replacing his or her principal residence but has not done so at the time of filing the annual tax return, a special statement must be attached to Form 1040 explaining this. There is no special form, however, to be used if replacement has not yet taken place. Instead, a brief statement is attached to the tax return. A typical statement is included, again, for the convenience of familiarizing the agent with the procedure. (A gain is to be prepared by an attorney or accountant.)

George Taxpayer
Social Security No. 000-00-0000

STATEMENT REGARDING SALE OF RESIDENCE
AND INTENT TO REPLACE

On December 19, 1977, I sold property located at 000 First Street, Los Angeles, California 90015, which I was using as my personal residence. The residence was sold for $65,000, less selling costs of $5,000, resulting in an adjusted sale price of $60,000. The basis of my personal residence at the time of sale was $40,000.

I have not yet replaced my old residence, but the time for replacement has not expired under the provisions of Internal Revenue Code Section 1034, and therefore, since I intend to replace the old residence within the time prescribed under said code section, I hereby elect to defer the reporting of the $20,000 gain on my 1977 income tax return.

The filing of this statement merely explains to the IRS why the taxpayer is not immediately paying the tax on the gain on sale of principal residence. Once the taxpayer replaces the old home with a new one, however, a second statement must be sent to the IRS explaining what has been done.

George Taxpayer
000 Main Street
Los Angeles, California 90017
Social Security No. 000-00-0000

June 5, 1978

Internal Revenue Service
Fresno Service Center
Fresno, California 93888

Re: Notice of Replacement of
       Residence under IRS Code Section 1034

Gentlemen:

On December 19, 1977, I sold property located at 000 First Street, Los Angeles, California 90015, which I was using as my personal residence. The residence was sold for $65,000, less selling costs of $5,000, resulting in an adjusted sale price of $60,000. The basis of my personal residence at the time of sale was $40,000.

On May 25, 1978, I purchased a new personal residence at 000 Main Street, Los Angeles, California 90017, for a total purchase price of $70,000. Therefore, I hereby elect to defer the reporting of the total gain on the sale in accordance with Internal Revenue Code Section 1034 and owe no additional federal income tax for the calendar year 1977.

Very truly yours,

George Taxpayer

Form 2119
(Rev. Oct. 1977)
Department of the Treasury
Internal Revenue Service

Sale or Exchange of Personal Residence

▶ Attach to Form 1040.

Taxable year

Note: Do not include expenses which are deductible as moving expenses on Form 3903.

Name(s) as shown on Form 1040
WINSTON TAXPAYER

Your social security number
000 : 00 : 0000

			Yes	No
1(a) Date former residence sold November 10, 1977		**(e)** Were any rooms in either residence rented or used for business purposes at any time? . .		X
(b) Have you ever deferred any gain on the sale or exchange of a personal residence?	Yes	No X	(If "Yes," explain on separate sheet and attach.)		
(c) Have you ever claimed a credit for purchase or construction of a new principal residence? . (If "Yes," see Form 5405.)		X	**(f)** If you were married, do you and your spouse have the same proportionate ownership interest in your new residence as you had in your old residence? . . . . (If "No," see the Consent on other side.)	X	
2(a) Date new residence bought November 20, 1977			**3(a)** Were you 65 or older on date of sale? . . . . (If "Yes," see Note below.)		X
(b) If new residence was constructed for or by you, date construction began N/A			**(b)** If you answered "Yes" to 3(a), did you use the property sold as your principal residence for a total of at least 5 years (except for short temporary absences) of the 8-year period preceding the sale?		
(c) Date you occupied new residence November 25, 1977					
(d) Were both the old and new properties used as your principal residence?	Yes	No X	**(c)** If you answered "Yes" to 3(b), do you want to elect to exclude gain on the sale from your gross income? . . .		

Computation of Gain and Adjusted Sales Price

4 Selling price of residence. (Do not include selling price of personal property items.)	**4**	65,000
5 Less: Commissions and other expenses of sale (from Schedule I on other side)	**5**	5,000
6 Amount realized.	**6**	60,000
7 Less: Basis of residence sold (from Schedule II on other side).	**7**	40,000
8 Gain on sale (subtract line 7 from line 6). If line 7 is more than line 6, there is no gain, so you should not make further entries on this form. A loss on the sale of a personal residence is nondeductible	**8**	20,000
9 Fixing-up expenses (from Schedule III on other side)	**9**	0
10 Adjusted sales price (subtract line 9 from line 6)	**10**	60,000

If you answered "No" to question 3(a) or 3(c), complete lines 11 through 14.
If you answered "Yes" to question 3(c), complete lines 15 through 17, or 15 through 20, whichever is applicable.

Computation of Gain to be Reported and Adjusted Basis of New Residence—General Rule

11 Cost of new residence	**11**	70,000
12 Gain taxable this year (line 10 less line 11, but not more than line 8). If line 11 is more than line 10, enter zero. Enter here and on Schedule D (Form 1040), in column f, line 1, or line 6, whichever is applicable .	**12**	0
13 Gain on which tax is to be deferred (subtract line 12 from line 8)	**13**	20,000
14 Adjusted basis of new residence (subtract line 13 from line 11)	**14**	50,000

Computation of Exclusion, Gain to be Reported, and Adjusted Basis of New Residence—Special Rule
(For use of taxpayers 65 years of age or over who checked "Yes," in 3(c) above.)

15 If line 10 above is $35,000 or less, the entire gain shown on line 8 is excludable from gross income. If line 10 is over $35,000, determine the excludable portion of the gain as follows:		
(a) Divide amount on line 10 into $35,000 . . . . |15(a)|		
(b) Excludable portion of gain (multiply amount on line 8 by figure on line 15(a) and enter result here) .	**15(b)**	
16 Nonexcludable portion of gain (subtract line 15(b) from line 8)	**16**	
17 Cost of new residence. If a new personal residence was not purchased, enter "None," and do not complete the following lines. Then enter the amount shown on line 16 on Schedule D (Form 1040), in column f, line 6	**17**	
18 Gain taxable this year. (Subtract the sum of lines 15(b) and 17 from line 10. But this amount may not exceed line 16.) If line 17 plus line 15(b) is more than line 10, enter zero. Enter here and on Schedule D (Form 1040), in column f, line 6	**18**	
19 Gain on which tax is to be deferred (subtract line 18 from line 16)	**19**	
20 Adjusted basis of new residence (subtract line 19 from line 17)	**20**	

Note: If you were 65 or older when you sold or exchanged your principal residence, and if that was your principal residence for 5 of the 8 years preceding the sale or exchange, you may elect to exclude part or all of the gain. If the property is held by you and your spouse as joint tenants, tenants by the entirety, or community property and you and your spouse file a joint return, only you or your spouse need meet the age requirement. You are only eligible for the exclusion once. This is true regardless of your marital status at the time you made the election.

Form 2119 (Rev. 10–77)

FIG. 1-3

Consent of You and Your Spouse to Apply Separate Gain on Sale of Old Residence to Basis of New Residence

Note: The following Consent need not be completed if there was no gain on the sale of the old residence. If, however, there was a gain, and if the ownership interests of you and your spouse in the old and new residences were not in the same proportion, the separate gain on the sale of the old residence will be separately taxable to you and your spouse unless this Consent is filed.

	Your portion	Spouse's portion
Adjusted sales price of old residence (from line 10)	$	$
Cost of new residence (from line 11 or 17)	$	$

The undersigned taxpayers, you and your spouse, consent to have the basis of the joint or separate interest in the new residence reduced by the amount of the joint or separate gain on the sale of the old residence which is not taxable solely by reason of the filing of this Consent.

Your signature	Date
Spouse's signature	Date

SCHEDULE I—Commissions and Other Expenses of Sale (Line 5)

This includes sales commissions, advertising expenses, attorney and legal fees, etc., incurred to effect the sale of the old residence. Enter the name and address of the payee and the date of payment for each item.

Item explanation			Amount
ABC Realty	11/20/77	Commission	$ 3,900
Legal Beagle, Esq.	11/01/77	Legal advice	500
XYZ Escrow	11/20/77	Escrow fees and closing costs	600
			$ 5,000

SCHEDULE II—Basis of Old Residence (Line 7)

This includes the original cost of the property to the taxpayer, commissions, and other expenses incurred on purchase, the cost of improvements, etc., less the total of the depreciation allowed or allowable (if any), all casualty loss allowed (if any), and the nontaxable gain (if any) on the sale or exchange of a previous personal residence.

Item explanation	Amount
Original cost	$ 35,000
Additional improvements	5,000
	$ 40,000

SCHEDULE III—Fixing-up Expenses (Line 9)

These are decorating and repair expenses which were incurred solely to assist in the sale of the old property, and which are not ordinarily deductible in computing taxable income nor taken into account in computing the basis of the old residence or the amount realized from its sale. Fixing-up expenses must have been incurred for work performed within 90 days before the contract to sell was signed, and must have been paid for not later than 30 days after the sale.

Item explanation	Date work performed	Date paid	Amount
			$

For more information obtain Publication 523, Tax Information on Selling or Purchasing Your Home, from your local IRS office.

☆ U.S. GOVERNMENT PRINTING OFFICE : 1977—O-218-300   25-0016750

In our examples, the taxpayer purchased a piece of property for a price higher than the adjusted selling price of the old principal residence, so that all of the gain was deferred. If the purchase had been for a lower price, a new calculation on Form 2119 with an amended tax return would have had to be filed and the tax on the gain paid at that time, plus interest.

If the taxpayer either fails to replace within the time period or intends not to replace, the IRS must be notified. In the event that the owner of a principal residence, for one reason or another, does not replace within the 42 months of time allowed as noted earlier, a letter or Form 1040X must be sent to the IRS explaining the situation. Accompanying the letter must be all the tax on the gain that was due when the principal residence was sold, plus interest at rates then in effect.

George Taxpayer
000 Main Street
Los Angeles, California 90017
Social Security No. 000-00-0000

July 15, 1978

Internal Revenue Service
Fresno Service Center
Fresno, California 93888

Re: Notice of Nonreplacement of,
Residence under IRS Code Section 1034,

Gentlemen:

On January 12, 1977, I sold property at 000 First Street, Los Angeles, California 90015, which I was using as my personal residence. The residence was sold for $65,000, less selling costs of $5,000, resulting in an adjusted sale price of $60,000. The basis of my personal residence at the time of sale was $40,000.

At the time I filed my tax return for the calendar year 1977, I elected to defer the reporting of the $20,000 gain on said sale. The time for replacing said residence has now expired; and I did not purchase a new residence within that time. I therefore enclose a check in the amount of $4,621 to cover additional income tax, plus interest, from the time of filing the 1977 tax return to the present date, along with an amended tax return for 1977.

Very truly yours,

George Taxpayer

19. When there is involuntary conversion, the taxpayer has 18 months after the conversion to replace property (or up to 2 years for new construction.)

Occasionally, a principal residence will be lost to the owner through no voluntary decision. Typically, this "involuntary conversion" occurs from destruction, theft (rare, but we have heard of a house that was stolen by house movers in Los Angeles), requisition or condemnation, or the sale or exchange of the property under the threat of any of these.

If that should happen, the owner has the full holding period under the nonrecognition on the sale of personal residence to replace the property and comes under the deferral rules.

20. No loss may be taken for tax purposes on the sale of a principal residence.

Unlike the sale of investment property, the tax law specifically excludes recognizing the loss on a principal residence.

2

Tax Deductions for Everyone on a Principal Residence

It has often been said that the only real tax shelter available to middle-income Americans (who form the majority of real estate buyers today) is their home. While this is not entirely true (many middle-income families also own second and third homes as true tax-shelter investments), the principal residence does afford its owner the opportunity to "write off" often large sums of money.

From a tax standpoint, it is advantageous to own rather than rent a principal residence.

As most agents are aware, interest paid on a mortgage is deductible from federal income taxes. Likewise are all property taxes. For a family that has a principal residence on which it pays $1,500 a year in property taxes

29

and $2,500 a year in mortgage interest, this means a deduction of $4,000 when federal taxes are figured. The benefit here can be put into perspective by comparing it with the family that rents instead of owning its principal residence (see Table 2-1).

TABLE 2-1 Renting versus Ownership of Principal Residence

	Family which rents	Family which owns
Income after normal deductions	$20,000	$20,000
Deductions for mortgage interest and taxes	—	4,000
Income on which taxes are paid	20,000	16,000
Tax bracket	28%	25%
Approximate tax	$ 3,484	$ 2,460
Saving because of owning personal residence	—	1,024

Assuming that both families make the same monthly payment, the family that owns its personal residence in our example is saving more than $1,000 a year in federal taxes compared to the family that rents.

The deductions that can be taken for investment property cannot always be taken for a residence.

Real estate held for investment purposes usually consists of a house which is rented out or an apartment building or perhaps even a commercial or industrial building. On a piece of investment property, most expenses may be used to offset income (and in some cases may be used to show a loss, preferably only on paper). Typically, maintenance, some repairs, depreciation, and some improvements fall into this category.

On a residence, however, these items *cannot* be deducted from personal income *unless* the owner can show some business usage of the home. (Improvements can be used to reduce any gain on the sale of the property.) For rules on business use of the home and limitations see Chapter 19.

Expenses can be used to reduce the taxable gain on the sale of a principal residence.

It is the wise agent who advises a client purchasing a principal residence to save all receipts for improvements to the property. When it comes time to sell, these receipts can form the basis for reducing the taxable gain on the property.

Let's say that Leona bought a two-bedroom home 20 years ago for $20,000. Yesterday, she sold for $60,000. Her gain, if for a moment we forget selling expenses, was $40,000.

Selling price	$60,000
Cost of residence	−20,000
Profit	$40,000

Taxes on the $40,000, even assuming capital gains treatment (discussed in Chapter 7), would take a sizable chunk of it.

If, however, Leona, over the course of her 20 years of ownership, had added a patio and deck, expensive shrubs, lawn, a new concrete driveway, a bigger water heater, a new and improved space heating system, luxury carpeting and drapes, and so on, she might have actually spent $20,000 on improvements (that's $1,000 a year for 20 years, a reasonable sum). At the time of sale, relying on her receipts to back up her claim, she could add the $20,000 spent in improvements to the $20,000 in cost of the residence, bringing her up to an adjusted basis of $40,000. Now when she sells for $60,000 (less adjusted basis of $40,000) she shows a gain of only $20,000. This substantial reduction in gain is accomplished by the fact that the improvements we noted earlier may be added to the original cost of residence *when gain is figured.*

COSTS OF SALE
In addition, many costs of selling may be subtracted from the sale price to further lower the gain. The largest of these, and an item which agents can't point out enough, is the *full commission.* In addition, the following expenses may be deducted:

1. Expenses of advertising
2. All escrow fees and filing fees
3. Legal services connected with sale
4. Legal services connected with title policy

Leona had $5,000 in allowable expenses, including the commission, to deduct from her $60,000 sale price, giving her an adjusted sale price of $55,000. Now subtracting the adjusted basis, we find her taxable gain is only $15,000.

Adjusted sale price	$55,000
Adjusted basis	−40,000
Taxable gain	$15,000

Of course, we said Leona bought the property for $20,000. Actually, we meant she bought it for $18,000 and the costs of purchase (the same as those listed above) were *added* to the purchase price to find the *cost of residence*. Purchase costs were $2,000, giving us the $20,000 basis. Every home buyer is likewise entitled to this calculation.

3

Today's Tax Shelters and Leverage

A large portion of this book deals with real estate as a tax shelter. The reason is simple — it is almost impossible to say anything about real estate without in the same breath speaking of tax shelters. They are part and parcel of buying property in the United States, more so since the Tax Reform Act of 1976 eliminated shelters from most other investments. Yet, in recent years, real estate tax shelters have had a bad name among many investors. True stories are often told of investors who put tens and hundreds of thousands into tax shelter "schemes" and received no return on their money and, in some real disasters, even lost all the money they had invested.

It is not hard to understand why someone who has been bitten by such an investment will be shy of tax shelters. Yet in such cases it was not the very nature of shelters that was at fault. Rather, it was the way in which the shelter was put together for the investor. There are bad tax shelters and there are good ones, and it is important not to discredit all shelters because of those that have gone sour.

While the risk of failure exists in any investment, good shelters have the strong potential to be successful and generate substantial income. In most tax shelters we've seen that have been financial disasters, however, the potential for success was never really there. These shelters were doomed from the beginning, and the initial year or two that they apparently were "healthy" before the collapse was in reality just an extended terminal illness. Just as in the body there are characteristics of good health and characteristics of bad, so too does the tax shelter exhibit economic good or bad health. For the agent and the investor it is critical to know the differences.

Since the mechanics of real estate tax shelters are handled later in this book, we'll touch here only superficially on their actual operations. What we're really concerned with are the economics behind the shelter. But first, let us consider in a general way what a tax shelter is.

A tax shelter as a paper loss.

It has been said that the great advantage of real estate over other investments such as stocks, bonds, commodities, and so on, is that in real estate you can lose more than you invest. While that hardly sounds like an advantage, the structure of taxation in this country frequently turns what seems logical, upside down. Let's look at this idea more closely.

We'll begin by considering how a business, in general, operates with regard to federal income taxes. In business, it is the case that you subtract the expenses of your business from its income *before* tax is calculated. It follows, therefore, that if your expenses are higher than your income, you won't have any taxes to pay. It is upon this premise that the tax shelter is founded.

Of course, this too sounds illogical, since it would seem that you would be slowly (or rapidly) going broke if expenses exceeded income. In business, this is usually true. In real estate, it is not.

For a moment, let us think of most people as businesses that operate with very few expenses. Most people derive income by working: computer operators, farmers, clerks, editors, and almost anyone who works for someone else fall into this category. Normally, the government allows only very specific limited deductions to such "working people." These are the items found on Schedule A of IRS Form 1040 (itemized deductions) and include such things as interest, taxes, some medical and insurance costs, and so on. Since most people's income far exceeds these allowable deductions, they have a lot of tax to pay.

When a person invests in real estate, however, he or she now opens a new business, one that can have many more expenses. Real estate expenses on investment property generally include maintenance, interest, property taxes, some repairs, some improvements, and depreciation. These expenses are first offset against any income from the property. If the property produces more income than it has expenses, there is a gain, and that is added to the individual's personal income. On the other hand, if a property has more expenses than income, it shows a loss, and that *loss is subtracted from the individual's personal income.*

If, for example, a person makes $10,000 in personal income from working after normal deductions yet also sustains a $10,000 loss from real estate investments, that person has *no income tax* to pay, because there is no net income.

Of course, the question remains, How can a person make $10,000 in regular income after deductions, lose $10,000 in real estate, and still survive? How does such a person live? The answer is that the money made in regular income is normally in cash. The money lost in real estate frequently is lost only on paper in the form of a depreciation deduction (see Chapter 5.) Unlike cash losses, paper losses may exist, for practical purposes, only on paper. They may not be money out of the investor's pocket (see Exhibit 3-1).

EXHIBIT 3-1   *A Business Person*

Income derived from working (salary or self-employed) $10,000	*Loss* derived from an investment in real estate $10,000

Income	$10,000
Loss	−10,000
Income on which tax is paid	$ 0

Real estate is one of the few investments in which a paper loss is possible. It occurs because the tax laws allow *depreciation* as a deductible real estate expense.

Depreciation can be used to create a paper loss.

Depreciation is easily defined. It is a loss in value from any cause. If you buy a car today and pay $8,000, you can be fairly certain that by next year your car will be worth only $7,000 or less. It has depreciated in value.

The government presumes the same thing occurs with real estate improvements (that is, the building, not the land): each year, a building is worth less. This, however, has certain business consequences. If the building is an investment, that is, if you get rental income from it, then as it depreciates in value, a certain portion of your investment is lost forever. This portion that is lost (calculated according to strict rules, as we'll see later) is deductible each year as an expense against the property.

For example, an apartment building may have deductible expenses that include property taxes, mortgage interest, utilities, maintenance, some repairs, insurance, and so on. Now to this list can be added an annual expense for depreciation.

Of course, there are few places in this country where real estate does in reality depreciate. Rather, in most areas it appreciates in value. That is how we get a paper loss. A real estate investment may lose money on paper because of depreciation for tax purposes yet at the same time make money by actual appreciation. (We'll discuss this further in subsequent chapters.) How this works can be clearly seen in an example (see Exhibit 3-2).

EXHIBIT 3-2   *How an Apartment Building Can Create a Paper Loss (Tax Shelter) to Reduce Its Owner's Income and, Thereby, Income Tax*

Income from rentals		$10,000
Expenses		
Mortgage interest	$ 5,000	
Property taxes	3,000	
Utilities	500	
Maintenance	500	
	———	− 9,000
Spendable excess income before mortgage principal		$ 1,000
ADDING DEPRECIATION		
Expenses	− $ 9,000	
Depreciation	− 2,500	
	− $11,500	
Income from rentals		$10,000
Total expense		−11,500
LOSS		($ 1,500)

It is possible to make a cash profit on a paper loss.

What should be carefully noted about the apartment building in Exhibit 3-2 is that it is not *operating* at a loss. The *out-of-pocket* expenses are only $9,000 (perhaps a few hundred more when mortgage principal is added), compared to a $10,000 income. Income exceeds expenses by about $1,000. It is only when depreciation, which is only a paper expense, is counted that the building shows a loss overall.

As we mentioned earlier, the $1,500 loss can now be used to offset $1,500 of regular income for the investor. This process of offsetting, or sheltering, regular income is a tax shelter. Of course, the $1,500 is subtracted from the tax basis of the building, which means that eventually, when the property is sold, presumably for a profit, it will come back as a gain. Then, however (assuming it was not due to accelerated depreciation, as discussed later), that gain will be a capital gain.

Some of the advantages of real estate ownership should be evident from our example: tax shelters plus tax-free cash. Yet we have not really gotten to the full benefit of real estate investments: *that you can lose more than you invest.*

The big advantage of real estate is that you can lose (on paper) more than you invest.

Since the 1976 Tax Reform Act was passed, in almost all types of investment other than real estate, the "at-risk" tax rule has applied. When you buy stocks, bonds, commodities, and so on, the *at-risk rule states that you may not claim losses for more than you invest.* It's much like gambling. You bet $10, and if you lose, all you can lose is your $10 bet. The at-risk rule, however, does not apply to real estate. It's as if your bet is $10 yet you can lose, on paper, $100.

Negative Losses

Since there is no at-risk rule for real estate, it is possible to invest, for example, $10,000 in an apartment building and then lose $10,000 a year for the next 10 years on the investment. At the end of 10 years, you will have lost $100,000 on a $10,000 investment (it is hoped, of course, that this "negative loss" is all on paper). If you are in only the 15 percent tax bracket, over the 10 years you will have received $15,000 in tax savings. Tax savings are money you would normally have to pay in taxes but now don't have to. If you are in the 50 percent tax bracket, you will have received $50,000 in tax savings. This is to say you can show a healthy profit in cash on your investment, all the while showing a loss on paper. (Of course, this catches up somewhat when the property is sold, as we'll see later.) Consequently, the more you lose on paper in real estate, the more it is possible to make from a tax standpoint. As we said, logic sometimes gets turned upside down by taxation.

The difference between good and bad tax shelters is in the investment-income-expense mix.

Let us now look at what makes the difference between good and bad tax shelters: the investment-income-expense mix.

There is a definite ratio between the amount of an investment in property and the size of the loss. For a given property value, the *less* the initial investment, the *greater* the annual loss. This can be clearly seen in an example (see Exhibit 3-3). Let us suppose we are buying a piece of property with a value of $1 million. We know that the annual income is $140,000 and the annual expenses, including depreciation, are $180,000.

EXHIBIT 3-3 *Million-Dollar Building*

Income		$140,000
Expenses		
Utilities	$ 8,000	
Property taxes	25,000	
Insurance	10,000	
Maintenance	7,000	
Mortgage interest	70,000	
Depreciation	60,000	
		180,000
LOSS		($40,000)

As we've seen, the building shows a paper loss of $40,000 because of depreciation. If we take depreciation out, the building actually shows a profit.

Income		$140,000
All expenses	$180,000	
Less depreciation	− 60,000	
		−120,000
PROFIT		$ 20,000

Now, let us look at it differently. What we've assumed about this building is that there is a substantial mortgage—in this case, a mortgage for 80 percent of the value ($800,000) with interest payments of $70,000. If, however, we had *paid cash* for this building instead of mortgaging it, we would not have this interest deduction and we would not show a loss on paper.

Income		$140,000
All expenses	$180,000	
Less mortgage interest	− 70,000	
		−110,000
PROFIT		$ 30,000

Even with depreciation, but without mortgage interest, we end up with a profit on paper.[1] Normally, anyone who pays cash for real estate and has no interest deduction cannot show a paper loss. *Interest is frequently the single largest expense.*

Of course, almost no one pays cash. Normally, as we've indicated, there might be a 20 percent down payment and an 80 percent mortgage. With such a mortgage, the interest expense contributes to creating the $40,000 loss.

Distorting the Mix by Increasing Interest

The question naturally arises at this point, how can the loss be increased? As we've seen in the upside-down world of real estate taxation, the greater the loss, the greater the tax shelter.

Most expenses, including depreciation, are fixed either by actual costs or by government rules. The only expense which can be manipulated to create a dramatic change in the overall expense picture is mortgage *interest.* It is possible to get additional financing — to put more or bigger mortgages on the investment.

For example, what if instead of putting 20 percent, or $200,000 cash, down, our investor puts only $100,000 cash down and takes out a $100,000 second, interest-only mortgage? The annual interest might be $10,000 a year. This interest is added to the expenses and directly increases the loss.

Income		$140,000
All expenses before second mortgage	$180,000	
Second mortgage interest	+ 10,000	
		−190,000
LOSS (was $40,000)		($ 50,000)

The more interest, the bigger the loss.

OVERLEVERAGING

What we're talking about, here, of course, is increasing our "leverage." It might be worthwhile to take a moment to make sure we understand the term. It relates to the use of the mechanical lever. Archimedes, the ancient Greek, is generally credited with saying, "Give me where to stand

---

[1] There is still an additional $30,000 in tax-free income, due to the $60,000 in depreciation. See Chapter 5 for a further explanation.

and I'll move the earth," by which he meant that a lever of the right length with a proper pivot can move any weight. Figure 3-1 illustrates this principle.

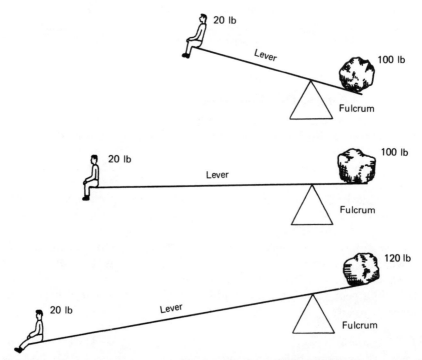

FIG. 3-1 The lever. By increasing the distance between himself and the fulcrum, a 20-pound boy can balance a 100-pound rock (or even 120 pounds) and eventually raise it higher than himself.

The analogy to real estate is striking (see Figure 3-2). With a big enough mortgage (the lever) from a lender (the pivot) you can buy a very expensive property (the boulder) with a small amount of money (the boy).

As we've seen, by increasing the length of the lever—the mortgage —an ever smaller percentage of money purchases the same building.

In the late sixties and early seventies, many well-meaning (and some not so well-meaning) agents and investors who were fascinated by the principle of leverage and who were looking for ways to increase loss on real estate investments wondered what would happen if the lever, or mortgage, were increased almost indefinitely. What if, to take our example in Exhibit 3-3, the apartment building were purchased with an $800,000 first mortgage and, say, a $175,000 second? The investment in the million-dollar building would be only $25,000. The results are

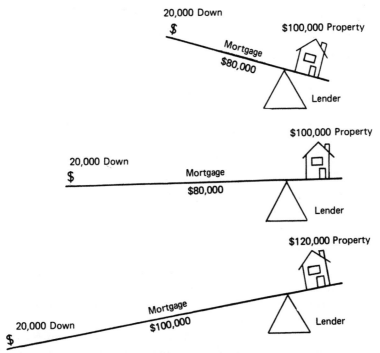

FIG. 3-2 Leverage in real estate. Essentially the same principle applies to both leverage in real estate and leverage in mechanics.

fascinating. There would be about another $17,000 in interest to pay increasing the loss to about $57,000. That's $57,000 loss in the first year on a $25,000 investment!

This meant that the investor who put up the $25,000 could deduct $57,000 from regular income in one year. If he or she were in the 50 percent tax bracket, this meant a saving of $28,500. The investor would have gotten back the entire investment plus $3,500 profit in the first year. It seems too good to be true (and it is), and a large number of investors plunged into such "bad" tax shelters.

What is wrong with this scheme is fairly obvious: each time the mortgage is increased, there's more cash needed to pay the interest. Any unusual expenses, such as emergency repairs, a big step-up in taxes, or a bigger-than-normal vacancy factor, quickly eat up the margin, which here is down to only $3,000. Typically, such financially unsound projects linger for a few years and then, in order to keep going, need infusions of new money from the owner (negative leveraging). When the owner balks at this, foreclosure results. A foreclosure in such cases can result in such strange things as a tax gain (explained in Chapter 14)! Some of this gain is usually counted as recapture of accelerated depreciation, which means some tax must be paid at ordinary income rates and not capital gains rate. The ultimate result is that the investor not only does not make a profit overall but loses money on the deal.

When the leverage, or the size of the mortgage, was increased, actual *cash* expenses were pushed beyond the ability of income to pay them, and the property lost money not only on paper, but also in actual cash. It is an ironclad rule of real estate that while paper loss may be beneficial, cash loss is not.

An interesting sidelight to this situation occurs if we go back to the mechanical lever in Figure 3-1, the principle on which the entire process is based. When we decrease the force moving the heavy weight by half (20 pounds to 10 pounds), we must *double* the length of the lever. Were we now to go from 10 pounds to 5 pounds, we'd have to double the lever length again. By the time we reach $2\frac{1}{2}$ pounds, or $2\frac{1}{2}$ percent of the weight of the rock, our lever becomes incredibly long. While in theory we can hypothesize infinitely long levers, in real life we cannot. Such a real lever would collapse or bend of its own weight. And that is exactly what happens in our bad tax shelter scheme—the project collapses because of the enormous weight of the mortgages.

Another point should be noted here. Beyond a certain reasonable limit, each time you reduce the investment by half, you are, in effect, doubling the risk of failure. This is what we meant when we said earlier that bad projects were terminally ill to begin with. They were so heavily leveraged that it was only a matter of time until they collapsed from the weight of their mortgages.

If the example we have looked at is a bad project, what then, is a good one?

How to Know a Good Tax Shelter
A good project is very simply one that is economically sound. By this we mean that it makes money (cash) instead of losing it *before* depreciation is added. The *mortgage-income-expense mix* is such that the building can show an economic profit. Our first example, with the building showing a $20,000 annual profit on a $200,000 investment before depreciation, is a healthy tax shelter.

Million-Dollar Building

Income	$140,000
Expenses, including an 80% or $800,000 mortgage but not including depreciation	−120,000
POSITIVE CASH FLOW	$ 20,000

This building shows a 10 percent annual excess income (positive cash flow) with depreciation not counted. To be safe, a project should show probably between 6 and 8 percent positive cash flow before depreciation. This mix allows for the unexpected, such as increased vacancy factors or unusual expenses. Most important, it allows for success.

In a good tax shelter, the investor will get some tax-free cash back each year and will also get some write-off against ordinary income. But most important of all, the investor isn't likely to go broke on the project. Remember, a loss in real estate is very desirable, but only as long as it is not out of your pocket.

4

Deductible Expenses
on Residential and Commercial
Investment Property

45

In new construction, some of the construction-period interest and taxes may be deducted immediately in the year in which they occur. page 52

On a personal residence there are basically only two deductions which can be taken—taxes and mortgage interest. On a piece of investment property many more deductions are available. As we noted in Chapter 3, technically speaking, these items are expenses which are used to offset investment property income. Besides depreciation (covered in Chapter 5), expenses which may be deducted from rental income on a dollar-for-dollar basis include interest, real estate taxes, maintenance and repairs, and incidental expenses, all described in this chapter.

Interest may be deducted as an expense.

The interest on the mortgage(s) is deductible and can be used to offset income. There is, however, a limitation on investment interest deductions under IRS Code Section 163(d).[1]

No prepaid interest may be deducted.

Occasionally, investors will ask how much *prepaid* interest they may deduct on a piece of real estate. What they are referring to are rules that no longer apply. At one time, years ago, it was possible for an investor to pay the interest on a real estate loan in advance of the time it was due. This was of great advantage to investors who happened to have a large income in a particular year. Since interest is deductible on a dollar-for-dollar basis, they could purchase a piece of property and pay all the interest on the mortgage (perhaps as much as 5 years') in advance, where the lender allowed. Since all the interest was deductible and since 5 years' worth could be a sizable amount, they could offset all the investment income and still have more interest expense left. This increased the loss on the property, which then could be used to offset regular income. In many cases, this offsetting allowed the taxpayer to avoid paying any income taxes at all in the year in question. The tax saved

[1] Under this code section, the total amount of interest an individual may deduct in a tax year is limited by a complex formula, the explanation of which is beyond the scope of this book. Taxpayers with large interest deductions should secure professional advice.

often made the inconvenience of paying interest in advance well worthwhile.

The government, however, looked upon the prepayment of interest as a way of distorting actual income, and so in the 1960s prepayment was limited to a period not to exceed 5 years. In 1969, the limit was reduced to 2 years and in the mid-1970s the limit became the year the property was purchased plus one full year. With the Tax Reform Act of 1976 prepayment was disallowed entirely. When an investor today asks how much prepaid interest may be deducted, the answer is none.

All real estate taxes are deductible.

As we mentioned earlier, all property taxes are deductible. This fact sometimes leads to an interesting method of creating a small tax shelter. It may be the case that a taxpayer has a windfall in a particular year and wants increased deductions in that year to help offset the increased income. One way of accomplishing this may be through advance payment of property taxes.

Advance payment of property taxes may create a small, temporary tax shelter.

In some areas, property taxes may be paid in two installments. In most cases, these installments fall in two separate years. (In California, for example, property taxes are due and payable half on December 10 and half on April 10 of the next year.) Almost everyone, naturally, waits until taxes are due before paying them and consequently makes two separate tax payments. However, if a taxpayer, for example, has an unusually high income in 1979 and wants increased deductions to offset it, then he or she can pay both installments (as the law usually allows) in 1979 and not wait until 1980 to pay the second half. The half of the tax bill paid in advance then is fully deductible in the year paid—a small but very effective tax shelter. (Of course, not having a second installment to pay will reduce the tax deduction the following year, but by then perhaps regular income will be lower.)

It should be noted that since property taxes are fully deductible whether the real estate is a principal residence or an investment, this method will work for all owners of any type of real estate.

All maintenance and repair work is deductible.

In general, all maintenance and repair work done to a piece of investment property is deductible on a dollar-for-dollar basis. Generally, the test to determine whether an expense fits under repair and maintenance is to show whether an item was simply fixed—either repaired or replaced— or whether the work actually resulted in an improvement or the addition of something new to the property. While this distinction may seem fairly simple on the surface, it is not simple in application. We have found that generally if the work done is very expensive, regardless of its nature, it may be considered an improvement to the property and not normal maintenance and repair.

The distinction between maintenance and repair and improvement is critical. Those items that fall into the first category may be expensed in the year in which they occur. Those in the second must usually be capitalized and depreciated over the life of the property.

All improvements to investment property must be capitalized over their useful life (only a portion of their cost may be deducted each year).

Henry owned a rental house that had air conditioning. The unit had been in the house for many years, and when it broke, Henry had to install a new motor and a new compressor. The cost was $850. He planned to simply subtract the full $850 repair expense from rental income that year, but his certified public accountant (CPA) cautioned him that he could not do that. Even though he was only replacing a worn-out unit, the cost of the new motor and compressor, in the government's eyes, would very likely constitute an improvement to the property. (The new parts, in theory, increased the value of the house.) Therefore, Henry had to capitalize the improvements. He felt that the motor and compressor would last 10 years, after which time they would have a scrap value of $50. He divided the $800 remaining value (after salvage) by the years and deducted $80 a year for the next 10 years using the straight-line method.

When is work repair and maintenance and when is it an improvement? Since many investors want as big a loss as possible on their real estate investments, the tendency is for the taxpayer to want to call all work and material costs "repair and maintenance." The government, however, wanting to prevent the taxpayer from distorting income through unreasonable repair and maintenance deductions, may want to call most such costs "improvements."

It is not always possible to determine quickly and easily whether an item is a maintenance and repair expense or whether it is an improvement. In questionable cases, the

taxpayer may have to prove that the item was not an improvement.

There are no hard and fast rules for determining what constitutes repair and maintenance. Each case must be decided on its own merits. We have found, however, that the following guidelines can be helpful. If maintenance involves what is normally considered janitorial work, it is usually deductible, as long as the cost is not unreasonably high. On the other hand, if "maintenance" involves, for example, reroofing the entire building or adding a deck, it probably is considered an improvement. If *repair* work costs $100 or less, it probably can be considered an expense and be fully deducted in the year it ocurs. Over $100, it probably should be capitalized. This, of course, can only be used as a "rule of thumb."

There are many exceptions, however. If the item being worked on is a very large and costly air-conditioning unit, then this guideline can be stretched. Perhaps Henry could have had his motor and compressor repaired at a cost of $200 instead of replaced. While the cost of parts alone may have been more than $100, in such a situation as this it might have been allowable to deduct the entire amount in a single year. On the other hand, if the plumbing also went bad on Henry's rental house and he had to replace a sink with a new one, for a total cost of $50, he would probably have to capitalize both the cost of the sink itself and the labor involved in installing it. As we cautioned, each case must be decided on its own merits.

Before we leave the subject of repairs and improvements, note should be made of what the relationship is today between the government and taxpayers on this point. Today, some taxpayers are calling very large items "repair and maintenance." Their approach is that if questioned by the IRS on the large deduction, they will seek to prove that the cost is not an improvement and that it deserves to be expensed in the year it occurred.

Let's take an example. Martha had the opportunity to buy an old reform school for half a million dollars. She was a wealthy woman and made the purchase. Then she spent another $500,000 rebuilding the structure, converting it into a commercial building. At the end of the year, she claimed the entire $500,000 in conversion costs as repair expenses, capitalizing none of it.

The IRS disagreed, saying that the entire $500,000 should be capitalized over the life of the building—some 20 years. This meant that in the first year Martha would get a deduction of only about $25,000 instead of the $500,000 she took. This matter never got to tax court. Out of court, the IRS settled by allowing Martha to expense $200,000 immediately and capitalize only $300,000 over the 20-year period.

This illustrates two points. The first is that the rules for determining what can be expensed immediately and what must be capitalized over a period of years are vague. If the taxpayer can reasonably show why an item should be expensed immediately, the government may agree. In this case, Martha indicated that she never went into the project with a plan of renovation. Rather, along the way of repairing the old building it occurred to her that it would change nicely into a commercial building. Most of the money she spent repairing. Only part of the money was actually spent renovating.

The second point is that experience has shown some taxpayers that occasionally it may be better to claim a large deduction and later settle for a smaller one in arbitration with the IRS than to make no claim at all. Of course, certain risks are involved here, including the possibility of being charged with fraud if the deduction should be very large and totally disallowed. No such action as that described above should be taken except on the specific advice of your accountant or tax attorney.

Incidental expenses may also be deductible.

In addition to the major expenses we've just covered, there are other costs in operating a rental property which also may be deducted. It is in the area of incidental expenses that quite often the taxpayer forgets to deduct items which may have cost a considerable amount of money.

1. Advertising. Advertising done to secure a tenant for a piece of rental property is fully deductible.
2. Utilities. All utilities paid by the owner for a rental property are fully deductible.
3. Gardening. All gardening work that is not an improvement is deductible. (Putting in a $500 oak tree, however, is probably understandably an improvement and would have to be capitalized.)
4. Management fees. Fees paid for managing a piece of rental property are fully deductible.
5. Other expenses. Any reasonable expense incurred in the operation of a piece of rental property that is not an improvement may be deducted. Here are tips on some that many people are not aware of or forget:
   a. Mileage from the owner's house or office to the investment property and back, on rental business, is deductible at 17 cents a mile.
   b. Any reasonable personal expenses with regard to trips to the investment property are deductible. If, for example, the property is 300 miles away, the cost of transportation (perhaps the owner flew both ways), as well as reasonable costs for meals, lodging, etc., is deductible.

c. Telephone expenses are deductible—that portion of the phone bill reflecting calls made for the benefit of the investment property.

d. Legal and accounting fees paid to another person for work on the property are also deductible.

An investment credit may be available on some *personal property* purchased as part of a real estate investment purchase.

In general, the investment credit is not available on *residential real estate*, unless the property is primarily rented out to transients. The credit's primary application is commercial real estate where the personal property is related to a business.

A tax credit is a sum of money deducted directly from the tax to be paid on income. A tax credit is a highly desirable item. Depreciation, property taxes, interest, and so on, as we have seen, are deductions—they are deducted from rental income and may thus create a loss. This loss may then be deducted from personal income. A tax credit is deducted directly from the tax to be paid to the federal government. In a sense, a tax credit reduces the bottom line of your income tax form. In terms of tax savings, therefore, each dollar in tax credit is often worth two, three, or more times each dollar in normal deductions, depending on the tax bracket. Needless to say, tax credits are much sought after.

The IRS allows an investment tax credit of up to 10 percent of the purchase price of personal property used in a business. In the purchase of a commercial building (a legitimate business) where the owner is the tenant and there is $100,000 worth of furniture, for example, this means the buyer can directly subtract from income taxes up to $10,000 (10 percent) in the year of the purchase. As should be readily apparent, this can be an important factor in helping an investor decide whether or not to make a purchase.

There are, however, certain conditions imposed on this investment credit. Where it applies to both *new* and *used* depreciable personal property, the personal property *must have a useful life of at least 3 years*. The tax credit is figured in this manner:

1. If the basis of depreciation is at least 3 years but no more than 5 years, the tax credit is $3\frac{1}{3}$ percent.

2. If the basis for depreciation is 5 to 7 years, the tax credit is $6\frac{2}{3}$ percent.

3. If the basis of depreciation is over 7 years, the full 10 percent credit can be claimed.

It must be noted that this tax credit is in the form of a bonus. It does not in any way affect the normal depreciation that can be claimed on the property. Even if you take the 10 percent credit, you still have 100 percent of the item left to depreciate.

If furniture is depreciated separately from the rest of an investment property, a special bonus depreciation may be allowed.

Very often, as we shall see in Chapter 5 on depreciation, an owner will depreciate the components separately from the shell. Even when this is not done, an owner may depreciate the personal property, such as furniture, separately from the real property. In either case, in the first year a bonus may be obtained.

All personal property that has a useful life of 6 years or more can be depreciated 20 percent at the time of purchase. This is a one-time-only deduction, and it has specific limits.

The limits on the bonus deduction are depreciation of 20 percent of the first $10,000 of value per taxpayer (or a maximum of $2,000) and depreciation of 20 percent of the first $20,000 of value in a joint return ($4,000).

It must be noted that, unlike the tax credit we were speaking of a moment ago, this depreciation bonus is subtracted from the remaining value of the item. If 20 percent of the value is deducted, only 80 percent remains to be depreciated over the useful life of the item. If, however, the limiting amount of this bonus has been reached, then only the maximum bonus depreciation is subtracted from the amount to be depreciated over the useful life.

In new construction, some of the construction-period interest and taxes may be deducted immediately in the year in which they occur.

In the past, it was possible for someone constructing a new apartment building to deduct immediately *all* the interest and property taxes as they were paid during the construction period. This proved a real boon to investors, since during this construction period there was no income, presumably, coming from the project. Without being offset by income, this interest and property tax expense constituted the equivalent of a total loss on the property. It could be totally written off against personal income, giving investors a very large deduction during the construction period. This write-off was, in fact, the reason why so many investors, with high incomes to shelter, went into the business of real estate construction.

In the 1976 Tax Reform Act, the government clamped down on construction interest and property tax expense. These can no longer be deducted as paid but must be capitalized and deducted over 10 years.

The 10-year amortization period is not effective immediately but will be phased in over three separate 7-year periods for each of the three types of investment property (nonresidential, residential, and low-income housing).

Table 4-1 shows the amortization period for construction-period interest and taxes paid, or incurred, during the years through 1988.

TABLE 4-1 Amortization Period

Year paid or incurred	Nonresidential years	Residential years	Low-income housing, years
1978	6	4	1
1979	7	5	1
1980	8	6	1
1981	9	7	1
1982	10	8	4
1983	10	9	5
1984	10	10	6
1985	10	10	7
1986	10	10	8
1987	10	10	9
1988 and thereafter	10	10	10

5

All about Depreciation

56

The agent who begins and ends a career in real estate selling principal residences is a rarity. Most agents move very quickly into the area of investment property.

The tax questions buyers of investment properties ask tend to be very different from those asked by those buying principal residences. They may include questions such as, "How much loss (tax shelter) will the property generate on paper?" or, "What is the positive cash flow?" An investor purchasing a commercial or apartment building may ask, "What are the advantages of depreciating the components separately from the shell?" while another may want to know, "How do I establish the basis for depreciation?"

Since tax considerations are such a vital part of buying investment property, the agent will need to know the answers to these questions and hundreds more in order to fully present the property's advantages to a potential investor. Long gone are the days when agents merely needed to know the price and loan terms to sell property.

In Chapter 4 we saw that for tax purposes it is helpful to think of a piece of investment property as a business that has both income (usually from rentals) and expenses. Real estate income is usually straightforward, taxwise: it is the total income received from rent. (We'll discuss some complications that arise here in Chapter 16.) What can sometimes be confusing, however, particularly to someone just learning about real estate and federal income taxes, is that there are at least two different kinds of income which are frequently discussed.

Real estate *investment income* is derived, usually, from rental of real property. *Regular income* is derived from a taxpayer's normal job or occupation.

For our purposes, we'll be considering taxpayers for whom real estate investment is a side activity. Such investors have a regular job, such as mechanic or teacher or engineer, and they only dabble in real estate. This distinguishes them from a "dealer" in real estate, who buys and sells property for a living. Many different rules apply to dealers.

The salary or income a person derives from regular work is usually termed regular, personal, or ordinary income. On the other hand, when that person buys a piece of real estate for investment purposes, that property produces its own rental income, which is quite separate and distinct from regular income. It produces investment income.

Certain items are deductible from investment income and certain items are deductible from regular income. But it is absolutely critical that what is deductible from one not be confused with what is deductible from the other.

In real estate, "expenses" are usually those costs of operation which may be deducted from the income of an investment property for the purpose of calculating annual profit or loss.

We'll go specifically into what expenses are allowable shortly. The important point to understand here is that expenses involved in operating a piece of property can be used to offset only rental or investment income. For example, if an individual owns a house that is being rented out and spends $10 advertising the property in the local paper, that $10 can be subtracted only from any income derived from the rental of the property. This may seem an obvious point, yet we've seen countless agents who mistakenly assume that expenses are directly deductible from regular income.

"Itemized deductions" are usually those items which the government allows the taxpayer to subtract from regular income before figuring income tax.

Everyone knows what "itemized deductions" are. They are medical payments (within certain limitations), residence mortgage interest and taxes, donations, and so on, figured on Schedule A of Form 1040, the individual income tax return. Another deduction, usually calculated on Form 1040, Schedule E, is the loss shown on the ownership of a piece of real estate. This loss, as we've just seen, is calculated by *first subtracting* all the expenses involved in operating a piece of property from the income. Any loss is then *deducted* from personal income. (Of course, if there should be a gain instead of a loss, then this would be added to regular income before income taxes were calculated.)

What can become confusing here are the terms. Expenses are *deducted* from rental income to get gain or loss on investment property. But loss on investment property can then be *deducted* from regular income. The word "deducted" can be used both when gain or loss on investment income is calculated and when tax to be paid on regular income is calculated. The important thing to remember is that the word is not within the exclusive domain of either calculation. Rather, it is simply a useful term. If it seems confusing, try this rule of thumb: Whenever figuring expenses and investment income, say that expenses are *subtracted* from investment income. When figuring income tax on ordinary income, say that losses from investment properties are *deducted* from ordinary income.

Of course, what we're talking about are two separate calculations.

The first is made to determine whether a piece of property made money (profit) or lost money (loss). Such a calculation is illustrated by Figure 5-1.

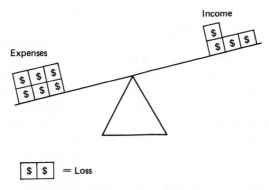

FIG. 5-1 **Investment property. Here we see that there are two units more of expenses than of income. This property lost money after expenses were subtracted from income.**

In Figure 5-2 we take the two units of loss and deduct them from a taxpayer's regular income. If the taxpayer makes 16 units of income, these two units of loss will reduce that income to 14 units. This is also frequently called "writing off," or "offsetting," income.

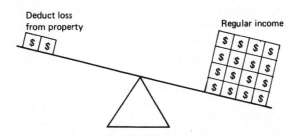

FIG. 5-2. **Calculating personal income tax. Loss from investment property helps reduce income from regular job or occupation.**

Now that we have explained income, let us move on to expenses. What we are concerned with in this chapter are strictly those expenses that may be subtracted from *rental* or *investment income* (although in looking into these we may also show how they can yield a loss that will then result in a deduction from *regular income*). For the remainder of this chapter we will be concerned exclusively with depreciation.

"Depreciation," for tax purposes, means lowering the value of an asset on paper by subtracting a certain portion from the value each year.

Textbooks often refer to depreciation as the loss in value of property from a wide variety of causes. These can be anything from physical deterioration to economic obsolescence. For tax purposes, however, depreciation has a slightly different meaning.

A piece of property, for tax purposes, is viewed as an asset. That asset has value—it has the potential of generating income. As the asset grows older, however, the potential for generating income diminishes. This can clearly be seen by comparing any two apartment buildings, one old and one new, in the same neighborhood. In general, the newer apartment building can command a higher rent than the older.

Eventually, as time passes and the asset gets older, it will diminish in value to the point where it can no longer generate income and must be scrapped. The period of time from when it is new until it is "used up" is the asset's useful life.

The government figures that during its useful life, an asset is a little less valuable each year until finally, as we've seen, at the end of its useful life it has only scrap value. The government, therefore, allows owners of such investment property assets to capitalize the asset's original value. Each year the asset is owned, a certain portion may be subtracted from the original value and subtracted from investment income. This is called "depreciating" the property.

While the concept of depreciation is fairly straightforward, its application can be complex. This complexity is due to the fact that there are at least three variables possible in depreciating real estate: Over what time period will the property be depreciated? What rate of depreciation will be used? What exactly will be depreciated?

The government was much more open to depreciation expense in the past than it is now, particularly with regard to the variables of rate and time. Very short terms of depreciation at very high rates were allowed. This meant that it was possible to show very large paper losses on property. This proved a boon for even modest investors. Not too many years back, for example, it was possible to depreciate used residential investment property for as short a term as 20 years at as high a rate as 200 percent a year (we shall discuss this 200 percent over 20 years in greater detail a little later).

Let us consider the hypothetical case of a grocery store checker, Ben. Ben bought a piece of investment property on which there was a new rental home, which he valued at $10,000. During the first year of ownership he used a 20-year depreciation term. This meant he divided the value by 20 years ($10,000 ÷ 20 = $500). And he used a 200 percent rate. Here he multiplied the figure resulting from the first calculation by 200 percent ($500 × 200% = $1,000). His first year's expense for depreciation was $1,000.

This $1,000 in depreciation expense could now be added to all the other expenses involved in operating the property and the resulting figure could be subtracted from rental income. All the other expenses totaled $900. Income was $800.

Other expenses	$ 900
Depreciation	+ 1,000
	$1,900
Income	$ 800
Less expenses	− 1,900
LOSS	($1,100)

Ben showed a taxable loss of $1,100 on the property in the first year of ownership. He now applied this loss as a deduction against his regular income. Since he happened to be in the 25 percent tax bracket, the loss was worth a saving to him of as much as $275 ($1,100 × 25%). This was money he would otherwise have had to pay in income tax.

You will recall that Ben's expenses other than depreciation were $900 while income was only $800. What we did not mention is that not all actual cash payments are deductions allowed against rental income by the government. The part of the mortgage payment that goes to principal is not deductible as an expense for tax purposes. This was another $50 a year. When this was added to the $900 of allowable expenses, the total actual cost of operating the property was $950.

Allowable expenses for tax purposes	$ 900
Other costs	+ 50
Total out-of-pocket expenses	$ 950
Less income from property	− 800
Money needed to be put back into property to keep solvent	$ 150

Before calculating depreciation, Ben was taking $150 a year out of his pocket and plowing it back into the property just to keep it going. This is called a "negative cash flow."

"Cash flow" is the direction money goes between an investment property and its owner *before* depreciation is calculated.

Positive cash flow is a flow of money from the property to the owner. Negative cash flow is a flow of money from the owner to support the property. *Cash flow is not affected by depreciation.* In Ben's case there was negative cash flow. However, if the expense and income figures were reversed, that is, if hypothetically there had been $150 more income than expenses, there would be positive cash flow.

Of course, Ben still did well because of depreciation. As we saw in Chapter 3, depreciation occurs largely on paper. When this paper expense was added to the other expenses, it boosted the total loss on the property to $1,100. (Remember, only $150 of this was actual negative cash flow—$950 was strictly on paper.) Because of this much larger paper loss, Ben was able to save, as we saw, about $275 on his income taxes. When this saving was balanced against the negative cash flow of $150, Ben came out with a cash profit of about $125.

What should be noted is that this profit was due to the very liberal depreciation rules allowed in the past. Today, Ben would not fare nearly so well. Today, on his new house, instead of a 20-year term, the shortest allowable term would normally be 40 years. This would cut his depreciation in half and completely eliminate the profit he could make from the property.

For many years this approach to handling depreciation on real estate continued, until Congress noted the great disparity between what the IRS allowed for depreciation and what was actually happening to property values. A diagram of this disparity might look something like Figure 5-3.

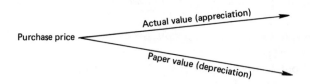

FIG. 5-3

Many members of Congress felt that because depreciation was almost always out of line with actual value, the government was in fact subsidizing the purchase of real estate investments. In favor of the then current system, it was pointed out that when a property owner sold, he or she paid taxes on the gain based on the depreciated value of the investment, not the original purchase price, and this took some of the sting out of the tax loss Congress was worried about. For example, if Ben sold after 1 year for $20,000 and his property had cost a total of $18,000, he would pay on a profit of $3,000, not $2,000.

Purchase price	$18,000
Less depreciation taken	− 1,000
TAX BASE	$17,000
Sale price	$20,000
Less tax base	−17,000
TAXABLE GAIN	$ 3,000

However, opponents of depreciation rejoined that, while depreciation ultimately was used to reduce the ordinary income of the investor, on sale in most cases tax was collected not at ordinary income rates but at lower capital gains rates.

The result of this debate has been a series of reform laws which over the years have restricted and reduced the depreciation allowed on investment real estate. Today, both the useful life of a piece of property and the rate of depreciation are based on guidelines which the taxpayer should follow. We shall see that these are far more restrictive than those in effect when Ben owned his piece of property. In addition, the government looks far more closely at what is being depreciated, that is, at how the value of the property has been determined.

DETERMINING BASIS

In the past many individuals arbitrarily gave a value to a piece of property and based the depreciation on that value. Seldom did the government require substantiation for the value. Today, substantiation is a necessity. But before we go into how to substantiate value, let us consider just what is depreciated.

Only improvements to the land may be depreciated—never the land itself.

Whenever we speak of depreciating property, we are speaking only of depreciating the house or the apartment building or the commercial building or whatever other improvements are on the land. Although these improvements diminish in value over a period of time, it is assumed that the land never diminishes in value (an exception to this rule is the using up of certain minerals, on which a depletion allowance is sometimes given).

For depreciation purposes, the value of a building is usually calculated from either its building cost, if new, or the price the taxpayer paid for it.

Since only the building is depreciated, a problem can arise here. If, for example, an investor pays $50,000 for a rental house, how does the investor determine which part of the $50,000 is for the building and which part for the land? In other words, how does the investor establish the tax basis for the improvement alone?

The *simplest* method of establishing basis for depreciation is to use the division between land and improvements found on the property tax bill.

Property assessors in most counties or townships in the country assess real property for the purposes of local taxation. These assessors almost always separate the real property into land and improvements. It has been our experience that when a taxpayer uses the assessor's separation as the method for establishing the basis on which a property will be depreciated, it is almost never questioned by the IRS. Perhaps it is simply the case that one tax assessor believes another.

Using the property tax bill, however simple it may be, may not be the most advantageous method for the use of the taxpayer-investor. The reason is that now the division between land and improvements more dramatically affects the amount of depreciation that can be claimed. The greater portion given to the building, the greater the amount to be depreciated. The less given to the building, the less there is to depreciate.

Since in most cases it is an advantage to get a big depreciation deduction in order to offset income from the investment and give the owner a tax shelter, it is in the taxpayer's interest to get the highest portion of the purchase price attributable to building and the lowest portion to land. (We will see later, however, that this can sometimes work against you when it is time to sell.)

As we have noted, a quick look at the property tax bill will show one allocation to land and another to building. Unfortunately, however, property tax assessors are notoriously prone to give excessively large allocations to land and small ones to building. Often the tax bill will show the land as 25 percent or more of the valuation when it really is 20 percent, 15 percent, or less. The five or ten percentage points' difference can mean a great deal when depreciation is figured and in some large projects can actually mean the difference between economic success and failure.

How, then, does the investor get the greatest possible allocation to building and the least to land?

In new construction, basis may be determined, for depreciation purposes, by computing the total cost involved in building the project.

Computing the total cost of new construction means keeping copies of records of every piece of material purchased, every bit of labor paid for. These records include phone calls, advertising, xeroxing of plans, and so on, in addition to what might be considered normal building expenses. When these costs are totaled and presented with the original purchase agreement for the land (under the assumption that it reflects the true value), the actual cost of the building and the cost of the land can usually be established to the satisfaction of the IRS regardless of what division between land and building the property tax assessor places on the project.

With existing buildings it may be possible to establish basis by writing into the sales agreement and related documents exactly what portion of the sale price the buyer is paying for land and what portion is being paid for improvements.

With existing buildings it is a bit more complicated than with new construction. Here it is frequently difficult or impossible to determine original building expenses. Further, if the building has been erected more than a few years back, chances are the original cost of construction is now a relatively smaller portion of an appreciated sale price. The answer is to come to an agreement with the seller on what portion of the sale price is being paid for land and what portion is being paid for building. This should be specified both in the sales agreement and in any later escrow instructions. While buyers, for reasons we have just seen, usually want almost all the sale price to be apportioned to building, sellers, on the other hand, frequently want a large portion attributed to land. The reason has to do with the seller's own basis for the depreciation used on the property.

Consequently, how building and land are to be apportioned can become one of the bargaining points, along with price and mortgage terms, in completing a transaction. In order to get a better split, buyers sometimes will be willing to pay more or make the financing terms more favorable to the seller. Getting an independent appraisal by a professional appraiser may satisfy all parties, including the IRS.

It should be pointed out that while this method can be used to offer proof for basis to the IRS, any outrageous allocation will undoubtedly only bring harm to the investor. No one is likely, for example, to believe that an investor bought a $300,000 apartment building paying $295,000 for the building and $5,000 for the land, even if buyer and seller both agree to it in writing.

DEPRECIATION RATES

As we mentioned, one of the big variables in depreciation has to do with the rate at which the property may be depreciated. There are two widely used methods for depreciating property today. The simplest to understand is called "straight-line."

For straight-line depreciation methods, a salvage value should be calculated before the depreciable value of the asset is determined.

Dolly purchased an investment home for $80,000, including land valued at $19,000. Since, as we saw when discussing the useful life of an asset, there is always a scrap value, Dolly figured a salvage value and subtracted it from the building value. This left building value at $60,000, the amount that could be depreciated.[1]

Purchase price		$80,000
Land	$19,000	
Salvage	1,000	
		−20,000
Building value		$60,000

Straight-line depreciation divides the number of years a property is to be depreciated into the basis. The resulting amount is subtracted each year from investment income as depreciation expense.

Dolly decided to depreciate the building for 30 years using the straight-line method. She divided 30 into $60,000, arriving at $2,000. Each year she planned to subtract $2,000 from rental income as depreciation expense. A graph of her depreciation would look like Figure 5-4.

---

[1] Whenever the straight-line method is used, the IRS requires that a salvage value be calculated. In actual practice, however, with property appreciating so rapidly, many investors figure no scrap value when calculating straight-line on real estate.

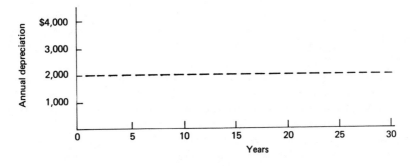

FIG. 5-4

As can be seen, the graphic portrayal of her depreciation, taking an equal amount out every year for 30 years, is a straight line; hence the name for this type of depreciation.

Since the straight-line method fully amortizes the depreciation over the useful life of the property in equal payments, it is considered the minimum depreciation rate, or the 100 percent rate. All other methods of depreciation calculate higher rates than straight-line.

When we are dealing with investment properties, as we have seen, paper loss is directly related to depreciation. The greater the depreciation, the greater the potential for a loss on paper. Consequently, getting depreciation sooner or "accelerating" it is frequently considered desirable. (Ben, in our earlier example, used an accelerated depreciation rate.) The most commonly used accelerated depreciation method is "declining balance."

In the declining-balance method of depreciation, an accelerated rate is applied to a straight-line method and the basis is recomputed for each year.

Most simply put, the declining-balance method simply multiplies a straight-line method by an amount somewhere between 100 and 200 percent. For example, when Dolly found out she could use an accelerated method, she immediately tried it out.

There is no need to compute a salvage value when using the declining-balance method.

You will recall that under the straight-line method Dolly figured a salvage value of $1,000 on her property. With the declining-balance method, a salvage value is already included in the method as part of the mathematics. (We shall go into this in a moment.) For the sake of comparison, however, let us assume that the depreciable value of Dolly's building is $60,000 with the declining-balance method, the same figure as for the straight-line method.

Under the straight-line method, Dolly divided a 30-year term into $60,000, arriving at $2,000 a year. To use the declining-balance method, she now began the exact same way. She divided 30 years into the depreciable balance, $60,000, and arrived at $2,000, only now she took this $2,000 and multiplied it by an accelerated rate of 125 percent. (The permissible rate is spelled out by the government. We will also go into rates in a moment.)

$$\$60,000 \div 30 \text{ years} = \$2,000 \text{ a year}$$

$$
\begin{array}{r}
\$\ 2,000 \\
\times\ \ \ 1.25 \\
\hline
\$\ 2,500
\end{array}
$$

Under this accelerated method in the past year she received $500 more depreciation than under straight-line. Since she was in the 25 percent tax bracket, this meant an additional saving to her of up to $125 she would have otherwise paid in taxes.

Naturally, Dolly was pleased with this method. However, upon reflection she realized that there was apparently something inconsistent here. If on the straight-line method she took $2,000 a year for 30 years, she would arrive at the $60,000 value she had estimated for her rental house. On the other hand, if on the declining-balance method she took $2,500 annually, at the end of 30 years she would have depreciated a total of $75,000, or $15,000 more than the building's value. How could that be?

In the declining-balance method the depreciation is recomputed each year on the basis of the amount not yet depreciated.

To avoid the possibility of depreciating more than the full value of a piece of property, it becomes necessary to go through all the calculation for each year of ownership. As we saw, in the first year Dolly could depreciate $2,500. For the second year she has to subtract this $2,500 of depreciation from the original value.

Declining Balance Step 1—Compute the Balance Not Yet Depreciated

$60,000
−   2,500 Depreciation taken
$57,500 Balance yet to be depreciated

This gives Dolly $57,500 yet to be depreciated. Now that she knows what is left to be depreciated, she goes through the entire process of calculating the depreciation.

Declining Balance Step 2—Divide the Total Years into the Undepreciated Balance

$$\$57,500 \div 30 = \$1,917$$

Declining Balance Step 3—Multiply the Result from Step 2 by the Accelerated Rate Being Used

Dolly must now multiply $1,917 by the rate she is using, 125 percent.

$1,917
×   1.25
$2,396

We see that the depreciation on the declining-balance method is lower for the second year than for the first (although it is still higher than for the straight-line method).

In each succeeding year Dolly must go through the entire procedure to calculate the depreciation she may take. In the third year, for example, she must do the following:

First, she must subtract the $2,396 taken in year 2 from the undepreciated balance.

$57,500
−   2,396
$55,104

Second, she must divide the resulting $55,104 by 30 years, the depreciation term she is using.

$$\$55,104 \div 30 = \$1,837$$

Third, she now must multiply the result obtained from applying a straight-line method by the rate she is using.

$$
\begin{array}{r}
\$1,837 \\
\times \quad 1.25 \\
\hline
\$2,296
\end{array}
$$

In the third year, she can take depreciation amounting to $2,296.

Since the amount of depreciation allowed each year declines with the undepreciated balance (hence the name of the method, declining-balance), it can be seen quickly that after a fairly short number of years the declining-balance method will start yielding less depreciation each year than the straight-line method.

Dolly planned to keep the property for a very long time and she didn't really need the increased paper loss created in the *short-term* by this method. Once she saw what would happen after a few years, she decided against the declining-balance method, and when she eventually filed her return she used the straight-line method. Which system an investor uses depends on his or her individual financial situation and is a fit subject of concern for that person's accountant or attorney.

The government allows specific accelerated depreciation rates on various types of property.

It is important to understand what rates of depreciation the government will allow. There are essentially three accelerated rates commonly used: 125 percent, 150 percent, and 200 percent declining-balance. Tables 5-1 and 5-2 indicate when each can be applied.

To see the actual effects of depreciation from both the straight-line method and the declining-balance method for the same piece of property, check Figure 5-5. This graph indicates all four rates for the same asset, a $120,000 piece of property depreciated over a 30-year term.

One further note about salvage value and the declining-balance method: You will recall we mentioned that it was not necessary to calculate the scrap value when using this method. The reason may be obvious now. Each time the depreciation is recalculated, a new balance is created. Although we are using a term of 30 years, it should be apparent that even if we calculated the process out to the thirtieth year, there would still be a small balance left. Using this system, you cannot decline the balance all the way to zero. This small balance left after 30 years hence remains, and may be accepted by the government, as the salvage value of the property.

TABLE 5-1

Types of realty	Maximum rates, percent
New residential rental housing acquired after July 24, 1969	200
Used residential rental housing, with useful life of 20 or more years, acquired after July 24, 1969	125
Used depreciable real property acquired before July 25, 1969	150
New depreciable real property, other than new residential rental housing, acquired after July 24, 1969	150
Used depreciable real property, other than residential rental housing, acquired after July 24, 1969	100

TABLE 5-2 Maximum Depreciation Rates, Percent

Residential		Nonresidential	
New	Used	New	Used
200	150 (if acquired before July 25, 1969) 125	150	150 (if acquired before July 25, 1969) 100 (if acquired after July 24, 1969)

While there are other methods of depreciating property, for all practical purposes, declining-balance and straight-line are the two types used almost exclusively in real estate. (See Appendix II for full depreciation tables.)

DEPRECIATION TERM

The final variable with depreciation is the term. It should be apparent that you will get much more depreciation *annually* if you depreciate a piece of property over 5 years than if you depreciate it over 50 years. (On a $10,000 property, after salvage value, depreciation over 5 years with the straight-line method is $2,000 a year. Over 50 years it is $200 a year.) Consequently, in order to get a greater depreciation annually, taxpayers tend to want a shorter term. On the other hand, the government, in order to avoid taxpayers' distorting their regular income through losses on investments arising out of unjustified depreciation,

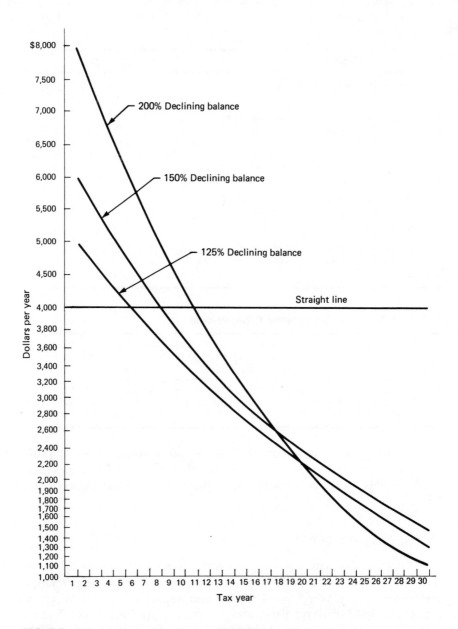

FIG. 5-5 **Depreciation methods on a $120,000 asset.**

tends to want longer terms. As of this writing, the exact terms allowable for depreciating real estate remain somewhat uncertain.

To aid taxpayers in determining how long (or how short) a term they may use to depreciate their property, the government came up with the asset depreciation range, or ADR, system. It gives guidelines for depreciating all types of assets, including some real estate. These guidelines, however, have extraordinarily long useful lives for real property. The ADR system guidelines, therefore, are rarely used by taxpayers for real estate. However, one provision of the tax law is that if a taxpayer elects to use the ADR for one asset, it must be used on all assets. If a taxpayer uses ADR for office furniture, for example, he or she then has to use it for real estate assets as well.

The important thing about the ADR system is that a taxpayer does not need to use it at all (except as noted above), if he or she can justify a different useful life of an asset. Justifying the useful life of a particular asset is once again within the domain of the tax lawyer or accountant. But, in general, we have found that the following guidelines for life spans for real estate have been helpful:

- New real property—30 to 40 years or more
- Used real property—20 years or more

(See Appendix II for full depreciation tables.)

DEPRECIATING BY THE COMPONENT SYSTEM

A glance at the guidelines makes it apparent that very long useful lives are the case, particularly for new property. However, while 40 years, to take a new building as an example, may be a reasonable length of time to figure a useful life for an entire structure, it may be an unreasonably long period of time for the internal parts or components. For example, electric wiring, elevators, plumbing, etc., may have a useful life of only 30 years or less.

It is possible to figure separate useful lives for the different components of a building (as well as one for the shell) and by their combination to come up with a shorter total useful life than if the building were considered as a single depreciable item.

The component system of figuring useful life is most frequently used in shopping centers and other commercial buildings. It can, however, also be used with good results in apartment buildings. While the actual setup of a component depreciation system will be discussed in Chapter 6 this is how a typical system might work for a new apartment building:

Component	Life, years
Shell	40
Electric wiring	20
Plumbing	20
Heating	20
Elevator	20

The net result is that although the shell retains its 40-year life span, by figuring shorter lives for the components, you can reduce the overall lifespan of the entire depreciable asset to, perhaps, 30 years or less. (It must be kept in mind that when the component method is used for figuring useful life, a salvage value must be given for each component. If, however, a declining-balance rate is used, the salvage value, as we have seen, is automatically computed as part of the mathematics.)

There are a variety of methods of figuring useful life. The government has an ADR system that suggests useful life for many things, including furniture. For components of apartment buildings, however, the ADR system has not often been used successfully by taxpayers.

We have seen several other cases where investors have attempted to establish useful lives by estimation based on their own calculation of the component's actual age in relationship to how many years of life it might have left. These have generally been defeated by the IRS. The only method we have seen that is successful is when an independent, competent appraiser is called in by the investor and he or she gives an appraisal of the value and the remaining useful life of a component. The IRS usually has been willing to accept the component system for investors where an appraiser has been used.

An agreement may be reached beforehand with the IRS on the depreciation allowed on a particular piece of property.

For some investors, the methods of figuring the rate, useful life, and basis for depreciation may seem too much like a case of outguessing the IRS. They may be worried that while it all looks good when the income tax return is filed, it could turn into a disaster if and when the taxpayer is audited.

For those who are particularly concerned about such an eventuality, it is possible to bring in the IRS at the time when basis and useful life are calculated and get the government's approval. This is done by means of a legally binding agreement regarding depreciation method, rate, and salvage value. Internal Revenue Service Form 2271 is used, and once the government signs, it cannot later challenge the taxpayer on these items.

Depreciation reduces the basis of a piece of property, but at sale it does not transfer with the ownership.

Although most agents are aware of this, it is worth repeating: Depreciating is not a gift to the taxpayer from the government.

As we saw in the example of Ben, each year's depreciation lowers the basis of the property. In Dolly's case, by year 5 she had depreciated her $60,000 building by $10,000 using the straight-line method. This meant her basis, after the depreciation, was actually $50,000. Were she to sell at the end of the fifth year, her gain would be figured on the adjusted basis, not the original value ($50,000, not $60,000). If she sold for $75,000, it would look thus:

Sale price	$75,000	Sale price	$75,000
Original value		Depreciated	
(if not depreciated)	−60,000	value	50,000
Gain on sale	$15,000	Gain on sale	$25,000

It should be clear that while depreciating property helps each year, it hurts when it comes time to sell. Of course, much of the sting is taken out of the tax bite on sale by the use of capital gains, which we go into in Chapter 7. The agent should pay special attention, however, to the fact that capital gains treatment may not be allowed on *all* the gain at the time of sale. A certain portion, primarily that part attributable to the use of an accelerated depreciation method, may become ordinary income on which regular tax is paid. Again, for a full discussion of recapture of depreciation, see Chapter 7.

While depreciation reduces Dolly's basis for figuring gain on sale, the sale itself wipes out all the depreciation. The next owner starts off fresh, as if the property had never been depreciated at all.

In our example, Dolly was depreciating a $60,000 property for 30 years. Since 5 years had elapsed when she sold, one might think, naturally enough, that there remained only 25 years of the original 30-year life to depreciate and that the new owner might begin at year 6 with the depreciated value of $50,000 that Dolly had as her basis when she sold.

That is not the way it is done. Rather, if an accelerated method is used, the new owner begins with a new basis, calculated on the purchase price

($75,000), and could begin, for example, with a depreciation term of 30 years. It would seem that in the process of a sale, the building in our example gained 5 years of life and $25,000 in value. Such is the logic of the tax law. The important thing to remember, however, is that depreciation does not carry over from one owner to the next. It starts fresh with each new owner.

MINIMUM TAX

After 1978 a minimum tax applies to the deducted amounts of capital gains and also to adjusted itemized deductions. In general, this minimum tax is payable only if it exceeds the taxpayer's regular tax liability; however, its calculation is complex and beyond the scope of this book. (It applies primarily to taxpayers with substantial incomes.) Taxpayers should consult their own accountants or tax attorneys in planning for this minimum tax and for its application in preparation of their tax returns.

It is always permissible to switch from an accelerated method to a straight-line method. Once the depreciation method on a piece of property is established, however, it normally takes IRS approval to switch from straight-line to an accelerated method.

You will recall in our example with Dolly that she chose to use a straight-line method rather than an accelerated method because she intended keeping the property for a long period of time and she saw that, after just a few years, she would actually be getting less money from the accelerated depreciation method.

An alternative which she did not consider, but which makes sense for many investors, is to use the accelerated method until the annual depreciation is about the same as it would be for the straight-line method and then to switch to straight-line. (Of course, a new calculation would have to be made based on the undepreciated balance left on the property.)

If the furniture is depreciated separately from the rest of the investment property, a special bonus depreciation may be allowed.

Very often, as we have already noted in this chapter, an owner will depreciate the components separately from the shell. Even when this is not done, an owner may depreciate the personal property, such as furniture, separately from the real property. In either case, in the first year a bonus may be obtained.

All personal property that has a useful life of 6 years or more can be depreciated 20 percent at the time of purchase. This is a one-time-only deduction, and it has specific limits.

The 20 percent bonus deduction is limited to the first $10,000 of value per individual taxpayer (for a maximum of $2,000) or the first $20,000 of value in a joint return ($4,000).

It must be noted that, unlike a tax credit, this depreciation bonus is subtracted from the value of the item. If 20 percent depreciation is allowed immediately, only 80 percent remains to be depreciated over the useful life of the item. Of course, if the maximum bonus depreciation has been reached ($2,000 for an individual taxpayer or $4,000 for two persons filing a joint return), then it is the limiting amount that is subtracted from the value to be depreciated over the useful life of the item.

SUM-OF-YEARS-DIGITS METHOD

Another method of accelerated depreciation permitted by the IRS in certain instances is the "sum-of-years-digits" method. It is mentioned here only in passing. In many years of working real estate we rarely have had occasion to use this method. Since it is complex, difficult to fully explain, and, in our opinion, seldom used in real property transactions, we have not included it in this book. The reader who wants a complete understanding of all types of depreciation, however, should consult other texts or IRS literature for a discussion of this method.

6

Walking through the Purchase of an Apartment Building: Tax Considerations

In previous chapters we considered the way in which expenses offset rental income to create a loss on investment real estate. We have seen how that loss can then be deducted from personal income so that it becomes a tax shelter. We've also seen just what expenses are allowable. But merely going over the rules may leave many readers in doubt as to how and when they are actually applied in the purchase of an investment property.

This chapter, unlike those preceding it, is a fictional case history. We will follow the story of Stephen as he buys a moderate-sized apartment building. His agent is Clair. She will first present him with justification for the price of the building. Then she will explain the costs involved in the purchase as well as the financing. Finally, she will consider the building from a tax standpoint. The way in which she handles this transaction will serve to illustrate just when and how tax considerations are likely to enter the picture in a real estate transaction.

Stephen had been in his medical practice only a few years when his father, a naval officer, died. Steve was left an inheritance of slightly more than $200,000. Steve, who had always been interested in real estate, decided the best investment he could make with the money would be to purchase an apartment building. He spent a considerable amount of time looking around until he found the building on Horizon Street. He liked the area, but now he had to decide whether or not it would make a good investment and whether or not he could make a real profit on his $200,000 by purchasing it.

The Horizon Street building had 35 units, all two-bedroom, and the building was 15 years old. Steve knew something about real estate, having once owned a rental house, but this was his first apartment building and he wasn't sure how to calculate price or return on his investment. It was the agent's role, however, to provide him with enough appropriate information to allow him to reach an intelligent decision.

The agent was Clair, and she was experienced in residential investment property. The first thing she pointed out to Steve was the difference when calculating price between a rental house and an apartment building. "In a house," she pointed out, "You try to find a comparable home and then use the comparable's selling price to establish the price for the house you want to buy. When you're buying an apartment building, however, you're really buying an income-producing business—a rental business. So, in order to figure price you need to know what the return on the investment will be. This is usually found by *capitalizing the net income.*"

Clair went on to demonstrate the formula used:

$$\text{RATE OF RETURN} = \frac{\text{Income}}{\text{Cost}}$$

"We need to know the net income, or the income after expenses but before the mortgage payment. Then we divide that by the price and we get the return on the investment. The lower the price and the higher the income, the greater the return.

"Once we find out the rate of return, we can then compare it with the return on other buildings to see if the price is reasonable, too high, or a steal.

"The problem with using this method, of course, is that we must first accurately know both the gross income and all the building expenses before we can find the net income and make our calculation. We must also have the same information for our comparables. For example, we would need this information for apartment buildings which recently sold on Vine Street, Memphis Avenue, and Charles Place. Quite frankly, I don't have that information and would have a hard time getting it."

Steve protested that this was too time-consuming and difficult a task. Clair agreed and then pointed out that agents and investors use a much more convenient, though less accurate, method of comparing price on investment buildings—the gross income multiplier. "This gives us a rough answer, since expenses are not figured in and they could differ between buildings, but it gives us a figure for instant comparison."

She explained it carefully. Gross income is simply multiplied by a number usually from 1 through 14. (These numbers are actually derived from comparisons between the gross annual income and the sales price of other comparable property recently sold.)

The number used as a multiplier is what determines comparable prices. For example, if apartment buildings in a given area are selling for eight times their gross income, then you simply multiply the income of the building you're considering by eight and that gives you the comparable price. If it turns out that the price asked is much higher, you can divide income into price to find out what multiplier is being used. For example, it may turn out that the owner is asking 10 times income, in which case you will probably want to pass. On the other hand, if only seven times income is being asked, it may be a terrific deal.

Steve was anxious to apply the multiplier to the building on Horizon Street. Clair said the apartment buildings in this area were generally using a multiplier of 8 to 9. She added that the annual income of the building was $125,688 (35 units with a 5 percent vacancy factor rented at an average of $315 per unit = $10,474 per month, or $125,688 per year). The asking price was $1 million. Steve quickly divided the gross income into the price and came up with a little bit less than 8.

"It's a good deal," he said.

"It's a good price for the area," Clair replied. "Whether or not it's a good deal depends on a lot more factors than this. It depends on the financing, the expenses, the condition of the building. and the tax advantages. They must all be considered before we know if it's a good deal for you."

Steve found that the financing was fairly simple. He would put down $200,000 from his inheritance and a lender would come up with a first mortgage of $800,000.

Closing costs which he would have to pay included:

1½ points on the mortgage	$12,000
Escrow fee and title insurance	3,000
Prorations of taxes, insurance, and rents	+ 6,000
	$21,000

Steve had enough money from his inheritance to take care of all these costs. Clair pointed out that points, escrow fee, and title insurance must all be capitalized over the life of the building.

"Now, let's consider your payments," Clair said. "The biggest single payment you'll need to make will be the principal and interest on the mortgage. We can expect to get a 9 ½ percent loan for 30 years." Using the handy calculating tables that all agents and most investors have (and that are available free from many lending institutions) she calculated a monthly payment of $6,725, or $80,700 per year.

"Now," Clair said, "let's add that in with all the other known expenses."

Mortgage payment	$ 80,700
Property taxes	22,000
Fire and liability insurance	8,000
Maintenance and repairs	+ 11,948
Total expense	$122,648

"Good Lord," Steve exclaimed, "the expenses are almost as high as the income."

Income	$125,688
Expenses	−122,648
Positive cash flow to owner	$ 3,040

Clair pointed out that thus far in their calculations, Steve would be making only about $3,000 a year on a $220,000 investment, or about a 1½ percent return on his money. "I'd be better off putting the money in the bank," Steve observed.

Clair told him to wait until all the calculations had been made before making up his mind. "We now have to figure your equity return. To do this we first assume that the building will not appreciate at all but will remain constant in value." Clair again went to her calculating tables to find the annual equity return on the mortgage (the amount of the loan payment that goes toward principal each year). For the first year it was $4,800.

"Let's assume you'll own the building for 5 years. Here's your equity return on the mortgage for the period of time."

First year	$4,800
Second year	5,600
Third year	5,600
Fourth year	7,200
Fifth year	+ 7,200
TOTAL	$30,400

Average return of equity over 5 years = $6,080

"You're going to receive back in equity about $6,000 for each year you own the building, assuming you keep it for 5 years. Remember, though, this is not in the form of cash—just equity."

When added to income from rentals the figures now looked like this:

Positive cash flow	$3,040
Equity return	+ 4,800
	$7,840

Steve pointed out that this was considerably better, since now he was making about 4 percent on his $200,000 investment, which was almost as good as putting the money in a bank. Clair pointed out that they were not through calculating.

Let's figures the tax shelter," she said. They started with the depreciation. "We'll put into the sales agreement that the building portion of the sale is $800,000 and the land portion is $200,000. This will give us the basis on which to figure depreciation of the building."

Clair went on to say that the current owner had hired an appraiser to give the value of the building before fixing the price. Along with the appraisal of the total building, the appraiser had also broken down the value and the remaining useful life of the components. She said that earlier that morning she had gone over the figures with her tax attorney and he had come up with a depreciation schedule based on the appraiser's work (see Table 6-1).

TABLE 6-1

Components	Value	Useful life, years
Roof	$ 20,000	10
Floors	80,000	10
Wiring	80,000	10
Plumbing	35,000	10
Elevator	20,000	10
Ceilings	50,000	10
Air conditioning	15,000	10
Furniture	50,000	8
Shell	450,000	20

"Since all the building components happen to have a useful life of 10 years, figuring the first year's depreciation is easy," Clair pointed out. "The $300,000 component value is simply divided by 10 years and then multiplied by 125 percent (the maximum for used residential property), giving us $37,500." She pointed out that since the declining-balance method was used on the components, it was not necessary to figure salvage value, as it would have been had straight-line been used (see Chapter 5).

"The first year's depreciation on the shell at $450,000 divided by 20 years' useful life and multiplied by a 125 percent declining-balance rate is $28,125. When we add the two figures together, we get a component and shell depreciation totaling $65,625. Finally, there's the furniture. In addition to the depreciation on the components and the shell, we can also depreciate the furniture [Table 6-2]."

TABLE 6-2

Furniture	Per unit	For 35 units
Carpeting	$ 600	$21,000
Drapes	300	10,500
Range & oven	300	10,500
Refrigerator	229	8,000
	$1,429	$50,000

Clair pointed out that the $50,000 worth of furniture, since it was used, could not be depreciated at the maximum rate of 200 percent allowed for new furniture. Rather, it could be depreciated at a maximum of 150 percent. Before getting to that she noted, however, that bonus depreciation of 20 percent of the first $10,000 of cost was allowed (a maximum of $2,000 bonus depreciation expense per taxpayer, $4,000 for a joint return; see Chapter 5).

"We take 20 percent of the first $10,000 and get $2,000 of depreciation. Then we use a 150 percent declining-balance at 8 years for the remaining value of $48,000 and get another $9,000. We add the $2,000 and the $9,000 to the $65,625 we've already figured for the first year and come up with a total depreciation for the first year of $76,625.

"Although we're just concerned with the first year, it's also important to see how depreciation will fare over the period of your ownership. We estimate you'll own the building for 5 years. Here's how the total depreciation will look [see Table 6-3]."

TABLE 6-3 Total Depreciation over the First 5 Years of Ownership

Year	Components, 125% for 10 years	Shell, 125% for 20 years	Furniture, 150% for 8 years
1	$ 37,500	$ 28,125	$11,000
2	32,812	26,367	7,313
3	28,711	24,719	5,941
4	25,122	23,174	4,827
5	21,982	21,726	3,922
	$146,127	$124,111	$33,003

"It's very important to know what depreciation is going to be beyond the first year to see if a dramatic change will affect the tax picture. For 5 years your average depreciation will be $60,648 per year. The biggest year will be the first, at $76,625. The lowest will be the last, at $47,630. In the last year you'll have $28,995 less depreciation than in the first, which could make a difference, depending on your tax bracket. But before we get into that, let's figure out deductible expenses versus income for the building."

Clair went on to add up all the tax-deductible expenses on the building for the first year:

Interest on mortgage	$ 75,900
Taxes	22,000
Fire & liability insurance	8,000
Maintenance and repairs	11,948
Depreciation	76,625
	$194,473

Clair pointed out that many repairs would need to be capitalized over the life of the item repaired, although it was possible to expense a good portion and deduct it in the year incurred (see Chapter 5 for details).

Deductions	$194,473
Income	−125,688
First year loss	$ 68,785

Clair now asked Steve what his income as a physician was. Roughly $75,000 a year, with about $11,000 of deductions, he answered. It put him in the 50 percent tax bracket.

Clair said that, in general, since the loss on the building in the first year was slightly greater than his adjusted gross income, the loss would offset his income and he wouldn't have to pay any tax on it. He would, however, have to pay a minimum tax on that part of the loss shown on the building that was due to accelerated depreciation.

This was figured in this fashion:

First-Year Depreciation

	Components	Shell	Furniture
Accelerated method	$37,500	$28,125	$11,000
Straight-line method	27,000*	20,250*	7,375*
Difference	$10,500	$ 7,875	$ 3,625

* Assuming salvage values of 10%. On the furniture, this salvage value is calculated on the full $50,000 before the bonus depreciation is subtracted.

Excess depreciation due to acceleration amounted to a total of $22,000

Components	$10,500
Shell	7,875
Furniture	3,625
Total excess depreciation	**$22,000**

A minimum tax may have to be calculated on this amount.

Clair said that instead of owing nearly $25,000 in taxes this year, if Steve purchased the apartment building, he would owe very little and could pocket the money he would otherwise pay. From the tax viewpoint, for the first full year of ownership he would receive:

Positive cash flow	$ 3,040[1]
Equity gain	4,800
Approximate saving on taxes from regular income	28,700
	$36,540

"On your investment of $220,000," Clair continued, "that means a return of about 17 percent the first year. And since you've got more depreciation than you need, the return could remain fairly constant for the 5 years you plan to own the building, barring unforeseen changes. We haven't even begun to calculate the increase you'll get if inflation boosts rents higher and increases your income (although this might be offset somewhat by higher property taxes)."

"It's a terrific deal," Steve said enthusiastically. "I can hardly wait to sign."

"It's not really that good," Clair commented. "In fact, I can't recommend it. Consider this. Although vacancy rates in most areas have been low, just a few years ago they were very high. The failure or change in location of a major industry, a recession, or any number of other factors can influence the vacancy rates, up or down, in the future. If the rate goes down and instead of having an average of two vacant units out of 35 you have only one or none, then that's all to the good. But what if it goes up? At $315 a month, for each additional unit that's vacant you would lose $3,780 a year in income. That means that just one more vacant unit, or about a 3 percent increase in the vacancy rate, can change your positive cash flow to a negative one [positive cash flow was $3,040]. Of course, as long as you continue to make your present income in your profession, such a negative cash flow of a few hundred dollars is trivial. But if something should happen—an illness, a lawsuit, or something else

[1] The cash here is tax-free, since the building shows a loss.

to prevent you from getting your income and taking advantage of the tax shelter afforded, that few hundred dollars could suddenly become very large.

"If we forget for a moment the tax shelter advantages of ownership, the building is basically unsound from an economic point of view. A mere 3 percent increase in the vacancy factor can eliminate the positive cash flow. What if there were 5 out of 35 units left vacant? That's a vacancy rate of only 14 percent. In many parts of the country this was considered typical only a few years ago. When five units are vacant, there is a loss of income of $11,340 as compared to only two vacancies. Balanced against expenses that means you'd have to come up with $8,300 a year out of your pocket just to keep the building. And that negative cash flow would more than wipe out any equity return you'd be getting.

"Considered by itself, unless the building is giving the investor at least a 6 to 8 percent return *before* tax shelter consideration, it is basically an unsound financial investment. Unless you can go into it anticipating to quickly be able to raise rents and thereby increase income, it doesn't make economic sense."

Clair looked at Steve. He was so intent in making out the deposit that he apparently hadn't heard what she had said.

7

How to Use Capital Gains

The purchase of real estate, as we have seen, offers the investor op-
portunities to receive tax-free income and to shelter some ordinary income during the ownership period. Eventually, however, investors sell
for one reason or another. At sale time, the very expense item that was
largely responsible for the overall tax shelter, the depreciation, can cause
the investor to be liable for a big federal income tax bite.

The basis of a real estate investment is lowered by all depreciation taken.

You will recall that when we were discussing depreciation (Chapter 5),
we noted that depreciation taken lowers the tax basis of the property.
For example, let's say that you purchase a piece of real estate in which
the building value is $100,000. You immediately begin depreciating it
and over a period of years depreciate a total of $60,000. You now have
an undepreciated balance left of $40,000.

Original basis	$100,000
Depreciation taken	− 60,000
Current basis	$ 40,000

At the time you sell the property, the current undepreciated balance
in our example ($40,000) represents the tax basis of the property. As
far as the government is concerned, it no longer makes any difference
that you purchased the property for $100,000. By depreciating $60,000
you have lowered that original basis to its current figure, and any gain
you make on the sale will be computed on the current basis.

If, for example, you were to sell your property for what you paid,
$100,000, it might seem to some that you need not have any tax liability.

After all, if you buy for $100,000 and sell for $100,000, you haven't really made any profit.

Purchase price	$100,000
Sale price	−100,000
Profit	$ 0

But, as we've said, gain on sale is not determined by profit. In fact, when taxes are calculated the word "profit" has no particular meaning. When calculating taxes we speak only of gain and loss.

For tax purposes, gain (or loss) on the sale of real estate is determined by subtracting the current basis of the property (after adjusting for improvements) from the sale price (after adjusting it for sale costs).

Any improvements that have been made to the property also have to be added to the basis. For our example, let's assume there have been no improvements. This leaves the current basis of the property at $40,000.

Basis after depreciation	$40,000

In a sale there are always some sales costs, such as commission, escrow fees, in some cases title fees, and so on. These are normally subtracted from the actual selling price, reducing it to an adjusted sale price. In our example, we shall let the closing costs amount to exactly $10,000.

Sale price	$100,000
Costs of sale	− 10,000
Adjusted sale price	$ 90,000

The current basis ($40,000) is now subtracted from the adjusted sale price ($90,000), giving the owner a gain of $50,000 on the sale.

Adjusted sale price	$90,000
Tax basis	−40,000
Gain on sale	$50,000

The owner in our example realizes $50,000 in gain on which taxes must be paid, even though no profit was made on the sale. It should be noted that, as was the case in figuring basis on a personal residence in Chapter 1, it makes no difference what the financing is on the sale. For tax purposes, all sales (except for installment sales with no more than

30 percent down in the first year and under other conditions described in Chapter 15) are considered cash sales.

Of course, today few people sell for the same price they paid if they purchased their property several years ago. Even so, the gain may still be considerably higher than any "profit." Let's say in our last example that the sale price was actually $150,000. Now the taxable gain on the sale (assuming no change in closing costs) would be $100,000.

Sales price	$150,000
Less closing costs	− 10,000
Adjusted sale price	$140,000
Less basis	− 40,000
Taxable gain	$100,000

Even though the "profit" on the sale was only $50,000 (sale price less purchase price), the gain was twice that amount.

Needless to say, the high gains on the sale of property, encountered largely because of depreciation, would discourage many investors from selling (and from buying) real estate if they were taxed as ordinary income. If, for example, an individual was making under $30,000 and, after deductions, happened to be in the 25 percent tax bracket, the sale of a piece of investment property and the accompanying gain at *ordinary rates* might prove an overwhelming burden.

If this person were fortunate enough to sell an investment property and realize $50,000 in gain and if this gain were now simply additional ordinary income and added to a current ordinary income of $30,000, it would produce a total ordinary income of $80,000. This would boost our investor into the 50 percent tax bracket or higher. Possibly as much as half and perhaps much more of the gain would have to be sent to Uncle Sam as tax. (This could be a particularly severe problem if there was no actual profit on the sale, as was the case in our first example.)

In most cases, however, gain from the sale of investment real estate need not be considered ordinary income. Rather, it can be considered capital gains and the taxpayer can take advantage of more lenient tax rates.

Capital gain in real estate is gain derived from the sale or exchange of investment property. Income from wages, royalties, interest, or similar sources is ordinary income.

It is important to understand that the capital gains laws, as they apply to real estate, refer only to the gain from the sale or exchange of investment property. Although it may seem obvious to many readers, care should be taken to figure the capital gains only on the total gain from the investment property — not the gain plus ordinary income. In our last example, a taxpayer received $50,000 in capital gain and had ordinary income of $30,000. The capital gains rule may be applied only to the $50,000 derived from the sale of the investment property. You may not first add the gain from investment property to ordinary income and then apply the capital gains rule to the entire amount.

Gain from sale of investment property	$50,000
Ordinary income	+30,000
Capital gains may not be applied to this amount	$80,000

For the capital gains rule, investment property is defined as a piece of real estate not used in trade or business but held for the production of income.

The definition has two tests to be applied to a piece of property. Both must be passed before capital gains treatment may be used. The first is that the property may "not be used in trade or business." This means that a "dealer" in real estate, or one who buys and sells property the way automobile dealers buy and sell cars, may not take advantage of the capital gains rule. Agents and investors must be very careful here, for the IRS frequently will determine who is and who isn't a dealer simply on the basis of how many properties are bought and sold in a year. Typically, a person who buys and sells five or more properties in a year is termed a "dealer in real estate" and would not be able to claim the advantage of capital gains treatment. This "five or more" rule, however, is not written in stone. It is open to interpretation based on a taxpayer's previous business record and the nature of what other business(es) the taxpayer may have. It is conceivable that a taxpayer who regularly bought and sold 10 properties a year and then had a poor year, buying and selling only three, might still be classed a "dealer." On the other hand, an individual who had a separate business and who bought and sold seven pieces of property in a year incidental to that business might still not be considered a dealer.

The second test of this rule is that the property must be held for the production of income. The production of income usually means rental income. For example, a piece of property on which there was a building rented out to tenants and which produced rental income would certainly fall within this rule. This would be the case whether the property in question was an apartment building or a commercial or industrial building. It would also apply to agricultural land on which the owner rented to tenant farmers.

Not all investment properties, however, qualify under this rule. For example, if an investor bought a piece of bare land and then immediately subdivided it, selling the parcels for a gain, the investor could not use the capital gains rule. The property was not purchased for the purpose of producing income; rather, it was purchased for the purpose of resale at a profit — something which does not come under capital gains.

From this discussion it may be concluded that the capital gains definition of investment property depends both on use and on time. If the property can be shown to be used for the purpose of producing income, the rule may be applied. This usually involves producing or attempting to produce some income. It also involves owning the property for a minimum specified period of time.

The minimum holding period for taking advantage of the capital gains rule is currently 1 year.

The federal government requires that an investor hold a piece of qualifying real estate for a minimum of 1 year in order to claim capital gains benefits. This holding period was much shorter in the past. In 1976 and earlier, it was only 6 months. In 1977 the period was lengthened to 9 months, and in 1978 it became 1 year. *Today in order to qualify for capital gains benefits the property must be held a minimum of 1 year.*

If both the property and the taxpayer qualify, the method of calculating capital gains is to find the total gain, take 40 percent of it, and add that to ordinary income. The other 60 percent is excluded but may be subject to a minimum tax for some high-income taxpayers.

The application of the capital gains rule is best seen through an example. Consider the case of Sally S., who purchased a house as a piece of investment property several years ago for $30,000. Sally added a fence to the house and a concrete driveway. Her total improvements came to $5,000. During the time she owned the property, she depreciated the house $10,000. (Note: Depreciation is calculated only on the improvements to the property, not the land. Gain on sale is calculated on both land and improvements.)

Original basis (cost of investment)	$30,000
Plus improvements	+ 5,000
	$35,000
Less depreciation taken	−10,000
Basis at time of sale	$25,000

When Sally sold her rental house, she received $50,000, and the total closing costs were $5,000.

Sale price	$50,000
Less costs of sale	– 5,000
Adjusted sale price	$45,000
Less basis	–25,000
Gain on sale	$20,000

Sally's gain on the sale of her investment house was $20,000. She had owned the property for several years, using it exclusively as a rental. Of course, she applied the capital gains rule. She took 40 percent of the gain and added that to her regular income:

$$\$20,000 \times 40\% = \$8,000 \text{ added to ordinary income}$$

Sixty percent of the actual gain was excluded, while 40 percent was included as taxable income for Sally.

For Sally, this worked out very well, for she had very little ordinary income. It is important to understand, however, that the capital gains treatment is on a sliding scale. If the $8,000 from the sale of the property were added to an ordinary income of $5,000, for example, it would mean that the taxpayer would be paying on $13,000. This might be near the 14 percent tax bracket, depending on deductions and credits. If, however, the taxpayer's regular income were higher, say $50,000, this $8,000 might boost him or her into a 40 or 50 percent tax bracket. If ordinary income were even higher, it might boost the taxpayer into even higher tax brackets.

Since in figuring capital gains, the nonexcluded portion of the gain on the sale of investment property is added on top of ordinary income, the effect is to boost the taxpayer into higher tax brackets. It should be apparent that the higher the income and the greater the gain, the less the advantage of capital gains.

Prior to October 31, 1978, capital gains was calculated differently.

A brief explanation of the old method of figuring capital gains is included here for the benefit of those who may have to deal with gains prior to the effective date of the new law. Prior to the Revenue Act of 1978, capital gains was calculated by using one of two methods. The first was the "regular" method and is identical to the method currently in use and described above, except that instead of a ratio of 60 percent to 40 percent of excluded capital gains to ordinary income, the ratio was 50 percent to 50 percent. Half was taxed as ordinary income and half was excluded.

The second was termed the "alternate" method. Here the taxpayer simply took the total gain, multiplied it by 25 percent, and then paid the full 25 percent as tax. In the case of Sally, with a $20,000 gain, the alternate method would look like this:

Total gain	$20,000
Alternate rate	× 0.25
Tax liability on the gain only	$ 5,000

There was one exception to the alternate method. When the total capital gain was $50,000 or higher, the taxable rate went up to a maximum of 35 percent on the amount above $50,000.

The Tax Revenue Act of 1978 *repealed* the alternate method of calculating capital gains.

A taxpayer in general may not use the capital gains rule for that portion of a gain on the sale of investment property which is due to the use of an accelerated depreciation method.

The federal government looks upon capital gains as a benefit to the taxpayer. It also looks upon accelerated depreciation (explained in Chapter 5) as a benefit. It will not allow a combination of these two benefits, except in certain cases which we'll discuss shortly. What this means is that, in general, if you use a straight-line method of depreciation, you'll have no problem with capital gains. If, however, you use a declining-balance or other accelerated method of depreciation, some portion of the taxable gain may not be taken as capital gains and instead may have to be taken as ordinary income.

To see how this works, let's consider the case of Harry H., who chose to use the declining-balance method of depreciating an apartment building he owned. Harry bought the property used, and so he applied the highest rate the tax law allows: 125 percent. The investment cost him $1 million, of which $800,000 was for the building itself. He applied the 125 percent declining-balance rate, at 20 years' useful life, to the $800,000 building as a whole. At the end of 3 years, he had taken depreciation expense of $140,820.

When it was time to sell, Harry found a buyer willing to pay $1,100,000, and a sale was concluded. The gain on the sale was calculated in the usual manner:

Original basis	$1,000,000
Plus improvements	0
	$1,000,000
Less depreciation	− 140,820
Current basis	$ 859,180

It cost Harry $75,000 in closing costs to sell the building, and so his adjusted sale price looked like this:

Sale price	$1,100,000
Less costs	− 75,000
Adjusted sale price	$1,025,000

Now, he subtracted his basis from his adjusted sale price.

Adjusted sale price	$1,025,000
Less basis	− 859,180
Gain	$ 165,820

Harry had hoped that he could apply the capital gains rule to all of this $165,820 gain. He was unhappy to learn from his accountant that this was not the case.

In order to figure what portion of his $165,820 gain was capital gains and what portion was ordinary income, it became necessary to determine exactly how much was due to the accelerated method of depreciation. The calculation itself is quite simple. We already know what the total depreciation from the accelerated method was for the 3 years Harry owned the building: $140,820. Now we simply calculate what Harry's depreciation would have been had he used the straight-line method:

Original value	$800,000
Term in years	÷ 20
Depreciation each year	$ 40,000
Number of years	× 3
Total depreciation taken if straight-line method had been used	$120,000

Using the straight-line method, Harry would have depreciated the property a total of $120,000. Now, we find what portion of his actual depreciation was due to the accelerated method.

To find what portion of depreciation was due to an accelerated method, subtract the depreciation for the same term that would have been taken by the straight-line method from the depreciation actually taken by the accelerated method.

Declining-balance method (accelerated depreciation method)	$140,820
Straight-line method	−120,000
Difference	$ 20,820

The depreciation that was due to an accelerated method is $20,820. This portion of Harry's gain will be taxed as ordinary income:

$20,820	Excess depreciation
× 0.70	Tax bracket (in Harry's case)
$14,574	Tax liability on ordinary income portion of gain

The remainder of the gain can be taxed under the capital gains rules.

This process of considering that portion of gain due to accelerated depreciation as ordinary income is technically called "recapture of accelerated depreciation" and is not to be taken lightly in the sale of property. Consider the consequences for Harry.

When the $165,820 gain on Harry's sale was reduced by the $20,820 that was due to accelerated depreciation, the resulting capital gain was $145,000. Harry was in the 70 percent tax bracket, and the ordinary income portion of his $145,000 was calculated in this manner:

$145,000	Capital gains income
× 0.40	
$ 58,000	Added to ordinary income

Since he was in the 70 percent tax bracket, his ordinary income tax on this taxable income came to $40,600.

	Taxed as ordinary income after
$58,000	capital gains calculation
× 0.70	Tax bracket
$40,600	Tax liability on capital portion of gain

Now the effects of recapture of depreciation can clearly be seen. On that portion of income recaptured, Harry (in the maximum 70 percent tax bracket) paid $14,574 on $20,820 of income. On that portion of income calculated under capital gains, he paid $40,600 on $145,000 of income. The rates are shown below.

Tax rate on portion of income due to recapture of accelerated depreciation:

$$\frac{\$14,574 \text{ Tax}}{\$20,820 \text{ Income}} = 70\% \text{ Rate}$$

Tax rate on portion of income reported as capital gain:

$$\frac{\$40,600 \text{ Tax}}{\$145,000 \text{ Income}} = 28\% \text{ Rate}$$

While Harry paid only 28 percent in tax on that portion of his income due to capital gains, he paid 70 percent in tax on the portion due to recapture of accelerated depreciation. Of course, the rates would be lower for lower tax brackets, but nonetheless, it is easy to see why recapture of accelerated depreciation became a very unwelcome item for Harry.

In certain cases, a portion of the recapture of accelerated depreciation may be forgiven.

Recapture of depreciation is a specialized subject, with many conditions and unusual cases. While what we've presented here should give the agent or investor some appreciation for how it works, the actual computation for a specific piece of property should be left to an expert. For example, depending on when the property was purchased, some "forgiveness" of recapture is allowed. For residential rental properties purchased after 1970, the forgiveness works as follows: None until the property has been held for 100 full months; then 1 percent of the accelerated portion is forgiven for each additional month of ownership. If the property is held 200 months, all that portion of depreciation taken by the accelerated method is forgiven and the entire gain may be treated as capital gain. The periods of forgiveness, however, vary for properties purchased prior to 1970.

The 60 percent portion of capital gains that is excluded from treatment as ordinary income is a tax preference item for some.

The 1978 Tax Revenue Act provided for a minimum tax on tax preference items. The excluded portion of capital gains (the 60 percent on which ordinary tax is not paid) is considered a tax preference item, but only when the taxpayer is required to use the alternative minimum tax method. However, since tax preference items normally affect only high-income taxpayers and since the rules for the minimum tax are quite complex, it is beyond the scope of this book to deal extensively with the subject. Readers concerned with tax preference items should consult with their own attorney or professional tax consultant.

8

Tax Problems and Solutions on the Sale of an Investment Property

In the preceding chapters we've covered many of the tax problems that are likely to be faced in selling investment property. Although we've tried to put them in logical order, to many readers new to federal income taxation and real estate they may sound like a jumble of unrelated parts. Perhaps the best way to see how they all work together is, once again, to take an example. Let's go back to our friend Stephen, who in Chapter 6 purchased an apartment building.

Steve went ahead with the purchase of the Horizon Street apartment building. He operated it successfully for 5 years, after which he decided to sell. He immediately became aware that if he sold for cash he would have a large tax bill.

You will recall that gain is computed by subtracting adjusted basis plus improvements from sale price less cost of selling (the same as for a principal residence, as in Chapter 1).

Steve bought the apartment building for $1 million. However, because of depreciation, his basis after 5 years was much lower than that. Only the building was depreciated (with separate useful lives for the building components, shell, and furniture). After 5 years, $303,241 had been depreciated, leaving an undepreciated balance of $496,759. When we add the original cost of land to this, we arrive at a basis of $696,759.

Original basis of building	$800,000
Less depreciation	−303,241
Adjusted basis of building	$496,759
Plus original basis of land	+200,000
Total adjusted basis	$696,759

Now we have to add in any improvements. As we noted in Chapter 4, it is often to the advantage of the investor to "expense" items rather than to capitalize them. However, many repairs or improvements are inevitably capitalized, and their cost, minus any depreciation already taken, is then added to the adjusted basis. In Steve's apartment building, this came to $25,706 before considering depreciation.

Basis	$696,759
Plus improvements	+ 25,706
Adjusted basis	$722,465

This adjusted basis is now subtracted from the sale price less any cost of selling. In this case, there was exactly $90,000 in expenses involved in the sale, including a real estate sales commission, escrow, title search, and other expenses. The total sale price was $1,340,000. The adjusted sale price was $1,250,000 after closing costs. When the adjusted basis is subtracted from the adjusted sale price, we see that Steve has a gain on the sale of $527,535.

Adjusted sale price	$1,250,000
Adjusted basis	− 722,465
Gain	$ 527,535

RECAPTURE OF EXCESS DEPRECIATION

Upon a cash sale, Steve would certainly use the capital gains treatment (see Chapter 7). However, he cannot claim all of his gain as a capital gain, because some of it was due to accelerated depreciation. You will recall that the portion of gain due to accelerated depreciation is treated as ordinary income. Table 8-1 shows the excess depreciation after 5 years for the Horizon Street apartment building.

From this chart we see that there is $66,991 of excess depreciation. This would be taxed to Steve upon sale as ordinary income. The remaining $460,544 of the gain on the sale, however, can be treated as capital gain. Let's see how this would work:

$460,544	Gain
× 0.40	
$184,218	Taxed as ordinary income

TABLE 8-1 Depreciation after 5 Years

Item	SHELL—original value $450,000. Depreciated at 125% for 20 years.	Components— original value $300,000. Depreciated at 125% for 10 years.	Furniture— original value $50,000. Depreciated at 150% for 8 years.	Total
Total accelerated depreciation	$124,111	$146,127	$33,003	$ 303,241
Total depreciation by straight-line method	101,250*	135,000†		236,250
Excess depreciation	22,861	11,127	33,003‡	66,991

* Assuming a 10% salvage value ($45,000).
† Assuming a 10% salvage value ($30,000).
‡ On furniture and equipment all depreciation is recapturable.

Under the capital gains rule, the $184,218 is now added to Steve's regular income. That means that his regular income is boosted by the amount both from the capital gain and from the recapture of excess depreciation:

$184,218   From capital gains
+ 66,991   Recaptured
$251,209   Taxable as ordinary income

Since this income is from a capital investment, it would boost Steve into the 70 percent tax bracket (70 percent is the highest tax bracket—in general 50 percent is the highest bracket if income is derived exclusively from personal service and not from capital investment). His tax on the gain would now be computed in this fashion:

$251,209   Taxable as ordinary income
×   0.70   Tax bracket
$175,846   Tax due federal government on
                          gain from sale of building

A tax of $175,846 is not a trifling sum. And when this tax is compared to the actual profit Steve would receive on a cash sale, it is even more onerous. Remember, he purchased the building for $1 million. When he sells for a million and a quarter (after selling expenses), his profit will be the difference between the purchase and sale prices, plus any increase in equity.

Sale price	$1,250,000
Less purchase price	−1,000,000
	$ 250,000
Plus equity return on mortgage	+ 30,400
Profit	$ 280,400

He will end up paying approximately $175,000 in taxes on an actual profit of $280,400. That works out to better than 62 percent of the profit in taxes. (Of course, it must be pointed out that during each of the five years of ownership, Steve received both positive cash flow and a tax shelter large enough to allow him to shelter his entire ordinary income.) Naturally, Steve, like any investor, would wonder if there were a better way than paying all the taxes upon sale.

There are several ways.

The first thing to consider, however, is the motive for selling. If the motive is to get out a large amount of cash, then perhaps a refinance might do better than an outright sale. If the property is now worth $1,340,000 (a figure based, presumably, on rent increases over the years—remember, in investment property, price is derived by capitalizing the net income or using a gross income multiplier), then a lender should be willing to loan 80 percent of the new value. An 80 percent loan would be equal to $1,072,000. After paying off the existing mortgage (after 5 years the balance would be $769,600), this would leave about $300,000 in cash (assuming no prepayment penalty). Expenses in obtaining the new financing, however, could be high. Nonetheless, Steve could probably get over $250,000 in cash out of the property by refinancing.

The advantage of the refinance is that there are no taxes to pay on the money, because it is borrowed. In a sense, Steve has use of the $250,000 tax-free *until* the time he eventually disposes of the property. (Note: He also should not have much difficulty in making the higher payments on the new loan, since rents, presumably, were increased over the 5 years in order to arrive at the new valuation.)

Perhaps, however, Steve's motive for selling is not to get cash out of the property, but rather to purchase an even larger property—one with the potential of delivering more positive cash flow to him. At this point, he might consider what is probably the most sophisticated of real estate transactions from a tax standpoint, the tax-free exchange.

9

An Introduction to the Tax-Free Exchange

Immediately selling property after it is exchanged
may endanger its tax-free status.   page 117

Improving property prior to an exchange may
threaten its tax-free status.   page 117

The tax-free exchange is one of the most useful real estate transactions, from a tax standpoint, both for the investor and the agent. It is, however, also by far the most sophisticated transaction. The following material, therefore, should only be viewed as a general guide explaining what a tax-free exchange is and showing the advantages and problems associated with it. *The reader is cautioned not to become involved in any actual tax-free exchange unless it is handled under the direct supervision of an experienced CPA or tax attorney.*

We'll go into the specific rules for the tax-free exchange shortly, but first let us consider when it should be used, what it is, and what it isn't.

As we mentioned in Chapter 1, probably the most common problem in understanding the rules of taxation for agents (and many investors) has to do with the deferral of taxes on the sale of a principal residence. Now, let us add that the second most common tax problem tends to be the confusion of the deferral rule on personal residences with a tax-free exchange. These are two totally separate areas of tax law, yet we have seen agents mix the two and apply the rules of one to the other.

The mistake is not a hard one to make. Federal taxation rules are at best difficult to understand. But the problem here, we believe, stems not from a difficulty in understanding the law but from a confusion of terms.

The deferral rule on principal residences is technically termed "non-recognition of gain on sale of principal residence." The tax-free exchange is "nonrecognition of gain on exchange." Both rules have in common the term "nonrecognition of gain," and therein lies the confusion. Let's examine more closely what this term means.

NONRECOGNITION OF GAIN

There are two types of gain—*realized and recognized.* First, let us consider "gain realized."

Gain realized is the price you sell your property for (less costs of sale) *less* its adjusted basis (the price you paid plus costs of sale and improvements and less depreciation, if any).

Gain is what you have made on the house for tax purposes. If you bought a house for $40,000 (after costs) and later sold it for $50,000 (after costs) and had no improvements or depreciation, your gain would simply be $10,000.

That is, your *gain realized* would be $10,000. But that might not necessarily be your *gain recognized*.

"Gain recognized" means that part of your realized gain the government recognizes for tax purposes.

Recognized gain is the amount of gain the government is going to tax — all, a part, or none. If in the above example the property were a principal residence and, following all the rules, you replaced it in the prescribed time period with another principal residence which had a higher purchase price than $50,000, none of your gain realized would be recognized. It would all be deferred to a later date.

On the other hand, if in the above example it were a rental house, on which you could not take advantage of the principal-residence sale-deferral rules, then probably all of the gain realized would be recognized and you would have to pay taxes on it.

A tax-free exchange is different from deferral of gain on a principal residence.

Both the deferral of gain on sale of a principal residence and a tax-free exchange offer *nonrecognition-of-gain-realized advantages*. But that is about all they have in common. The rules for these two types of transactions are completely different. Let us consider three of the major differences, shown in Table 9-1.

There are, of course, many other differences between the two sets of rules, but these are probably the most outstanding. What the agent and investor must understand is that the deferral of gain on a principal residence applies to principal residences *only*. The tax-free exchange applies to property held for investment or business use *only*. The two are not interchangeable. The only thing common to them is, as we have mentioned, the fact that gain realized may or may not be recognized.

TABLE 9-1 Deferral of Gain on Sale

Principal residence	Tax-free exchange
Maximum of 42 months' waiting period available to taxpayer.	*No waiting period usually allowed.* See page 133.
Used on principal residence only. May not be used on property that is held for investment (except that portion of investment property which is used as principal residence).	Used for investment property or property held for business use. *May not be used for principal residence.*
Property may be sold for cash.	Property must be *traded* for other qualified property.

Besides that, the rules are completely different. Applying the rules for one to the other can result in a real estate tax disaster.

ADVANTAGES OF A TAX-FREE EXCHANGE

If an investor sells a piece of investment property for cash and there is a gain on the sale, the investor will have to pay tax on that gain. On the other hand, if an investor trades that piece of property for another property and meets all the requirements under the rules for a tax-free exchange, then the gain on the sale (which may be the same as for a cash sale) may sometimes not be recognized, but instead may be deferred until the investor eventually sells the second property for cash. (Of course, our investor could continue deferring by exchanging tax-free the second piece of property for a third, and so on.)

This deferral opportunity is the big advantage that a tax-free exchange offers over a cash sale. It allows the investor to "step up" more easily (a step-up simply means buying a more valuable or higher-priced piece of property). It should easily be seen that if you sell a piece of property you currently own and pay taxes on your gain, you have less money to invest when you buy your next piece of property. On the other hand, if there were some way you could put off paying taxes on the gain from your sale (have it not recognized), then you would have more money available to invest in your next piece of property. You could take a bigger "step-up."

There are several other reasons why people use exchanges in general and tax-free exchanges in particular. These include:

1. The leverage on an existing property may be bad because of the appreciation in value over the years. The investor may not want or be able to refinance, yet the existing loan may only be a small percentage

of the property's value. By exchanging, the investor may acquire property with a higher mortgage-to-value ratio.

2. Agents frequently favor exchanges over sales if the owner of a piece of property has put an inflated value on it and refuses to consider a reduction (for practical reasons an exchange of properties at inflated prices may psychologically satisfy the owner). In addition, real estate agents have the opportunity of collecting two commissions on an exchange instead of one on a single sale.

3. An exchange may solve the problem of getting financing in a tight market. Since equities are exchanged and loans assumed, it may not be necessary to obtain a new loan.

Given these reasons for wanting a tax-free exchange, the next question is, Just what is it? It is an exchange of properties wherein at least one party does not pay tax immediately. We'll go over the specific tax rules in just a moment, but first let us see just what an exchange itself looks like.

In a cash sale, a purchaser buys a piece of property from a seller. A diagram of the transaction might look something like Figure 9-1.

FIG. 9-1

In simple exchanges, instead of a buyer with cash and a seller with property, there are two parties both of whom have property. (For a moment, we'll assume a perfect trade with no cash involved.) A diagram of an exchange might look like Figure 9-2.

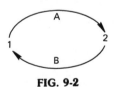

FIG. 9-2

In our diagram, 1 and 2 are the different properties and A and B are the different parties. At the beginning of the exchange, A owns property 1 and B owns property 2. During the exchange, they swap properties, and once it is completed, A owns property 2 and B owns property 1.

An Introduction to the Tax-Free Exchange **109**

What could be simpler? In terms of exchange, nothing. What we've discussed is a simple trading of properties without going into the tax problems involved. This simple two-party swap is often called a "double."

There are variations of the double. For example, let us suppose that instead of two parties, there are three involved, as in Figure 9-3. Now instead of a double we have a "three-cornered exchange."

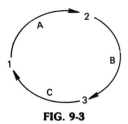

FIG. 9-3

Once again the numbers represent different pieces of property and the letters different parties to the deal. At the beginning of the transaction A owns 1, B owns 2, and C owns 3. During the transaction they swap in a clockwise motion. At the end of the transaction A owns 2, B owns 3, and C owns 1. (Again, we're assuming a perfect trade with no cash.)

This process of musical chairs with property can obviously continue for as many participants with properties as are willing. For example, similar four-cornered and five-cornered exchanges might look like Figure 9-4.

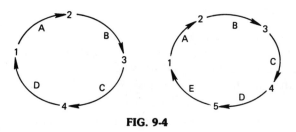

FIG. 9-4

The types of exchanges we've been diagraming thus far are called "circular" exchanges. They are extraordinarily simple, because each party has a piece of property that he or she wants to trade with another party. While this type of exchange is quick and easy to understand, unfortunately in real life it rarely occurs. Seldom do we find a group of property owners in perfect harmony, all willing to exchange what they have for what someone else has.

As we noted earlier, there are many reasons for wanting a tax-free exchange. But they all tend to come down to two: an investor wants such an exchange to gain a leverage or tax advantage, or an agent wants such an exchange in order to make a deal that otherwise could not be made. Consequently, there also happens to be two major types of exchanges that are not circular like those we've thus far seen. These might be labeled the "tax-payer's exchange" and the "agent's exchange," the second of which we'll discuss in Chapter 12. What makes them different from the circular exchange we've seen is that these last two usually involve cash.

A taxpayer's exchange usually begins when the taxpayer owning property 1 is looking around for another piece of property to trade for. The taxpayer may have as a motive any of three likely reasons we saw earlier: a desire to get a property with a better mortgage-to-value ratio; easier financing; or a step-up without immediately paying taxes on gain (which is the most common reason). Our taxpayer's approach is to look at properties listed for sale. Eventually, he or she may find one that seems suitable. As is most often the case, the investor who owns the desired property 2 does not want to exchange but instead wants to sell for cash.

As we'll see in a moment, the rules for a tax-free exchange have specific restrictions on any cash flowing through such an exchange, and so our taxpayer must deal with this problem: how to obtain property 2 without directly paying cash to an investor who refuses to trade. Our solution to this problem is the taxpayer's exchange. In it our taxpayer now puts his or her property 1 up for sale for cash.

Eventually a cash buyer comes by. We'll call this cash buyer for property 1 the "exchanger," for reasons that will become apparent very quickly. The exchanger anticipates a straightforward purchase of property 1, but our taxpayer informs the exchanger that there is a slight problem: our taxpayer does not want to sell for cash.

The exchanger may at first be outraged. Why advertise for a cash sale if cash is not wanted? Our taxpayer soothes the temper of the exchanger and says that he or she (the taxpayer) has already found a desirable property to trade for: it is property 2, owned by the investor.

At first, the exchanger does not see the connection. What does the investor's property 2 have to do with property 1? The exchanger simply wants to buy property 1 for cash.

The taxpayer suggests that the exchanger can get the desired property 1 but will have to make a little detour first: the exchanger will have to first purchase property 2 from the investor. Then, once the purchase is completed, the exchanger will have the property that our taxpayer wants and a trade can be made. Graphically the transaction might look something like Figure 9-5.

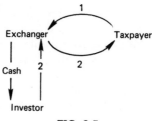

FIG. 9-5

It should be evident that this type of exchange is quite different from the circular exchange we were discussing earlier. Rather than a circle, we now have a triangle which is open at one end (see Figure 9-6).

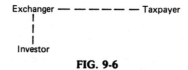

FIG. 9-6

What brings the investor and the taxpayer together, the pivot, so to speak, is the exchanger. This is the third party whom the investor has brought in in order to make the deal. It should be noted that in this transaction there are two separate steps. First, the exchanger buys from the investor the property that our taxpayer wants. Then, in step 2, the exchanger trades property 2 to our taxpayer for property 1.

The exchanger is the third party in our transaction who makes the trade possible. At this state, a reader might reasonably ask, Why does the taxpayer go through such a difficult procedure? Why not simply sell property 1 to the person we've labeled the exchanger and then buy property 2 directly from the investor? The answer is that our taxpayer is trying to avoid having any cash flow through the exchange, for reasons we will go into shortly.

These are graphic portrayals of the most basic types of exchanges — the circle and the triangle. Later we'll go into a four-cornered, square, agent's exchange, but for now let us look at the rules that make tax-free exchanges possible.

RULES FOR THE TAX-FREE EXCHANGE

Since the tax-free exchange is more sophisticated than the other real estate transactions we've been considering thus far, it tends to be a little bit more difficult to understand. But, it is not hard. There is no real estate agent or investor who cannot understand the rules for a tax-free exchange if he or she makes an effort. And the time used learning them will be well spent, since a familiarity with the exchange may be essential in bringing buyer and seller together. However, while the rules given here are basic to most tax-free exchanges, there may be many other considerations for any specific piece of property. Therefore, an agent or investor who has not before handled a tax-free exchange, or who is not thoroughly competent in them, should enlist the aid of an attorney when arranging such an exchange.

Definition

The rules for what makes an exchange tax-free occur primarily under Section 1031 of the IRS Code. Section 1031(a) states,

> No gain or loss shall be recognized if property held for productive use in trade or business or for investment (not including stock in trade or other property held primarily for sale, nor stocks, bonds, notes, choses in action, certificates or trust or beneficial interest, or other securities or evidences of indebtedness or interest) is exchanged solely for property of a like kind to be held either for productive use in trade or business or for investment.

Sections 1031(b), (c), and (d) go on to define gain and loss from exchanges in kind and also define how basis is established.

Although the general rules for the tax-free exchange take up no more than a paragraph, it will take a bit more than that to come to an understanding of them. Consequently, we'll take them one step at a time.

An "exchange" means that one piece of property *must* be transferred in return for another piece of property.

The sale of a piece of property for cash only does not constitute an exchange, even though the property is in a sense "exchanged" for cash. Sometimes a transaction that is really a cash sale may be disguised as an exchange, in which case it may not be recognized as tax-free. For example, a seller might agree to sell a factory to a buyer and then to buy another factory site as part of the transaction. This would be a cash sale and then a purchase, not an exchange of a factory for a new site. under the rules.

The property to be exchanged must be held for productive use in trade or business or for investment.

It is necessary here to differentiate between property held by a dealer in real estate and that held by a nondealer. This is the same distinction we ran into when defining whether a piece of property came under capital gains treatment back in Chapter 7. If the property being transferred is that of a dealer, the general rule is that no tax-free exchange is allowed, although it is possible that if the dealer *holds it for a long period of time*, it may be shown as an investment and a tax-free exchange may be allowed.

A further point is to distinguish between property held solely for sale and that held for investment. If the property that is exchanged is then immediately resold as part of a plan of liquidation, then it is a cash sale and not an exchange. An interesting case once involved a piece of property taken by a bank through foreclosure and then offered for resale at a later date. Since the bank's sole purpose in holding the property was to resell it, there was no tax-free exchange allowed when the property was transferred, but instead it was considered a cash sale.

The average investor often gets into trouble here with bare land. Suppose an investor trades for a large tract of land and then subdivides it with the intention of immediately reselling. The investor here probably does not qualify under the tax-free exchange rule.

It is important to distinguish between property held for use in trade or business, such as a building and land owned by an auto repair shop, and that held by a dealer whose business is primarily buying and selling real estate. In the case of the auto repair shop, the property is incidental to its regular business, while in the case of the dealer, the business is the ownership and sale of property.

Finally, some confusion occurs with regard to farmland. An unharvested crop, when it is part of a farm being exchanged, does qualify as property held for use in a trade or business. Yet, a residence on an exchanged farm, when it is for the personal use of the owner and not for the use of tenants working on the farm as caretakers or employees, may not qualify.

Property exchanged must be of "like kind."

The words "like kind" are critical to a tax-free exchange, since they determine what kind of property qualifies for an acceptable exchange. On the surface, "like kind" seems an easy enough definition: an apartment house for an apartment house, a farm for a farm. The term does, however, have subtleties which must be considred.

"Like kind" refers to the nature or character of the property and not to its grade or quality. This means that a particular kind or class of property may not be exchanged tax-free for property of a different kind or class. Under this definition, *it usually makes no difference whether the property is improved or unimproved* — such a distinction relates only to the grade or quality of the property, not its kind.

The real problem occurs when there is an exchange of real property for personal property. *Realty may not be exchanged for* personalty under the tax-free exchange rules we are considering. This means that while an apartment building can be exchanged for bare land and an old car exchanged for a new car, a piece of bare land may not be exchanged tax-free for an automobile.

Each case must be decided on its own merits.

The most common problem here (although we'll go into some not so common ones in a moment) occurs with regard to leases. A lease in general is in a kind of no-man's-land between real and personal property. For tax purposes, however, the lease has a more settled status. In considering a tax-free exchange, if the lease is for 30 years or more it is considered to be the equivalent of a fee title. For less than that period of time it is not considered equal to ownership of real property. For example, an exchange of a leaseback (immediately leasing the property back from the new owner) for real property when the lease is for more than 30 years may qualify as a tax-free exchange.

As we have said, improved property often may be exchanged for unimproved property, so that an investment property with a house on it may be exchanged tax-free for a lot which the taxpayer intends to build on or hold for investment. However, a rental house may not be exchanged tax-free for bare land when the intention is to subdivide and sell the bare land.

Some other tax-free exchanges of like kind real estate which normally may be made are listed here. (The reader should check with an attorney for any questionable exchanges.)

1. Rental house or apartment building for ranch.
2. Real property for water or mineral rights (allowed in those states where water and mineral rights are considered real property).
3. Unencumbered timberland for unencumbered timberland of an unequal quality and quantity of timber is allowed if properties are to be held for investment.
4. Property in the United States for property in a foreign country.

(Although we'll come to it in a moment, it should be noted that an entire transaction is not disqualified from tax-free status if some personal property is included in addition to a trade of realty for realty. Realty plus personalty for realty *may be partially allowed.*)

Some transfers which usually may not be tax-free are:

1. A motel for a nightclub
2. Timberland for the right to cut and remove timber on other land where such rights are personalty under state law

It should be noted that certain types of property are specifically excluded from a tax-free exchange. These include stock in trade or other property held primarily for sale, stocks, bonds, notes, choses in action, certificates of trust or beneficial interest, or other securities or evidence of indebtedness or interest.

Any "boot" in a tax-free exchange is taxable.

The word "boot" is derived from a slang expression, "to boot." It is something thrown into a transaction to equalize it. For example, if you were buying a new car, the dealer might throw in a new radio "to boot." In a real estate exchange of property, the "boot" is usually cash thrown in to equalize the transaction. If Fred were buying a free and clear $300,000 apartment building from Helen and giving in exchange a free and clear $250,000 apartment building, he might throw in $50,000 in cash "to boot." The $50,000 Helen received would equalize the difference in equities and it would technically be called the "boot."

Boot is also a critical term in an exchange, and it is essential that every agent and investor become thoroughly familiar with it and its subtleties. The reason is that while an exchange of properties may be tax-free, *boot* is taxable.

In a tax-free exchange it is frequently helpful to speak of "qualifying property" and "nonqualifying property." Qualifying property is simply those items which when exchanged do not incur a tax liability. In a real estate exchange, the qualifying property is the real property itself.

Nonqualifying property is simply those items which when exchanged incur a tax liability. In a real estate exchange they include cash and any personal property thrown in. In other words, nonqualifying property is boot and as such is taxable.

Boot does not necessarily disqualify an entire transaction from tax-free status.

That portion of gain realized on a transaction received in the form of boot is recognized. The remainder is tax-deferred.

For tax purposes in a tax-free exchange, any mortgages either assumed or taken "subject to" are considered to be boot.

If you were to trade even a million-dollar apartment building which had an $800,000 mortgage on it (your equity being $200,000) for another person's free and clear $200,000 lot and that other person assumed your mortgage or bought subject to it, your boot would be $800,000!

The reasoning behind this is straightforward. If you own a million-dollar building and have an $800,000 mortgage on it, you are liable for payment of that debt. If, however, someone purchases that building in a trade and takes over payment of that mortgage, that person has, to a degree, relieved you of your liability. It's the same as if that person paid you $800,000 in cash and you then used the money to pay off the mortgage. (Of course, not all boot is taxable—see next chapters.)

The application of a tax-free exchange status to a sale is mandatory. No loss may be recognized on a tax-free exchange.

If all the requirements of a tax-free exchange are met, for tax purposes the sale will be considered a tax-free exchange. Therefore, a taxpayer who wants to have a loss recognized should take great care to avoid a sale which can be treated as a tax-free exchange.

Immediately selling property after it is exchanged may endanger its tax-free status.

If property which is exchanged tax-free is then immediately sold, the government may contend that there was no intent to hold the property for investment but the intent was merely to sell. In such a case the tax-free status of the earlier exchange may be disallowed.

Improving property prior to an exchange may threaten its tax-free status.

Occasionally, it will be the case that a property owner will need to construct improvements to his or her property in order to arrange an exchange. This does not in itself defeat the tax-free status of the exchange, provided that the exchange has not begun. If, on the other hand, the other party to the exchange is obligated to make the exchange prior to construction or becomes directly involved in the construction it may result in loss of tax-free status. As long as it can be shown that the improvements were made in order to allow the *property owner to be in a position to arrange an exchange* there should be no problem.

These, then, are the elementary rules of the tax-free exchange. There are other rules and we'll consider many of them in the following chapters. But, in order to see how the exchange actually works, let's take an example.

10

A Step-by-Step Exchange and Some Rules

A TAX-FREE EXCHANGE EXAMPLE

Stephen wanted to sell his apartment building, but he didn't want to pay all the federal income taxes that came with the sale (check Chapter 8 to see what those taxes are). Since his purpose in selling was to buy a bigger piece of investment property, he began investigating the idea of a tax-free exchange. He was aware that if he met all the requirements, it would be possible to defer any gain on his present property when he traded for another.

Steve located a commercial center owned by Betsy. It had a fair market value of $2 million. He was enthused. If he could get Betsy to trade with him, he could "step up" and put his entire equity into the new property and not have to immediately pay any tax on his gain on the old property.

Unfortunately, for Steve to step up, it would be necessary for Betsy to "step down." She would have to go from a $2 million commercial center to a $1.25 million apartment building. While it is very easy to find investors who want to step up, it is almost impossible to find investors who want to step down. Betsy simply couldn't see any reason for trading for Steve's property, particularly since she had an equity of $1 million.

Betsy's commercial center:

Fair market value	$2 million
Mortgage	−1 million
Equity	$1 million

Steve, who by this time had become quite sophisticated in his real estate knowledge, pointed out how easily a trade could work. She would get a new 75 percent loan of $1.5 million on her property. She would get the proceeds of the loan, from which she could pay off her existing mortgage and have half a million to boot in cash. And, in addition, Steve would give his property in trade to make up the other 25 percent of the price. The trade proposed by Steve is shown in Exhibit 10-1.

EXHIBIT 10-1

Steve		Betsy	
$ 500,000	Equity	$ 500,000	Equity
1,500,000	First mortgage dispensed as follows:	750,000	Assumes loan on Steve's property
	$ 500,000 Cash to Betsy		
	1,000,000 Pays off existing mortgage		
$2,000,000		$1,250,000	

To Steve, it seemed a clear-cut case for a trade. He would get the commercial property he wanted. Betsy would get $500,000 in cash plus Steve's property.

There were just two things wrong with it, which Betsy's agent pointed out. First, while it undoubtedly would work fine for Steve from a tax viewpoint, it would not be a tax-free exchange for Betsy. The tax laws are not based on an investor's equity in the property, but on price less basis. Betsy would realize an enormous gain on the sale, most, if not all, of which would be recognized. She would undoubtedly have to pay hundreds of thousands of dollars in taxes. Of course, this would be no more than she would pay on a cash sale. The point was that the exchange offered her no advantage. (If she had been willing to use an installment sale, it is just possible she might have been able to save money on taxes. See Chapter 15.)

Second, Betsy had no desire to trade for an apartment building. She didn't want to step down; she wanted to get out. She wanted to get her money out of her commercial center, put it into the bank, and retire. She simply *did not want* to trade at all.

This is typically the real estate situation prior to a tax-free exchange. One party wants to trade to a stepped-up piece of property without paying tax on the transaction. The other party does not want to step down but frequently wants to step out. (It's also a fact of tax-free exchanges that when there are just two parties to the exchange, one usually benefits, taxwise, and the *other frequently suffers.*)

Betsy's agent, Mary, came up with the solution to this problem — a three-cornered exchange.

A Three-Cornered Exchange

A three-cornered exchange would bring a third party into the transaction, and everyone could then hope to get the desired result. Mary, the agent, explained the problem this way. Steve wanted the commercial center, but Betsy did not want the apartment building, only cash. The solution was to find a cash buyer for the apartment building. That way the new buyer's cash could go to Betsy, getting her out as she wanted.

Mary drew a diagram of the deal she proposed (see Figure 10-1). The new cash buyer would purchase Betsy's commercial center, partly cashing out Betsy. Then the new cash buyer could trade the center to Steve for the apartment building, getting Betsy the rest of her cash. The cash buyer would end up with the apartment building, Steve with the center, and Betsy with all cash.

The agent eventually came up with such a cash buyer, Bill Sherman. Bill was willing to buy the apartment building for the fair market value of $1,250,000, putting down $250,000 in cash and taking out a first mortgage for the $1 million balance.

FIG. 10-1

It was at this point that Mary used the utmost tact to carefully explain the transaction to all the parties involved so that each thoroughly understood what was happening. She began by explaining why the deal might look confusing.

She pointed out that there was a difference in equities — Steve had $500,000 in equity, Betsy had $1 million. There was also a difference in value — the apartment building was worth $1,250,000, the commercial center, $2 million. And, finally, there was an apparent shortage of cash — Bill only had $250,000 to put into the deal, yet there was a full million required to cash Betsy out.

Equities

Then Mary indicated that all these apparent problems could easily be solved. First, she explained the difference in equities by going back to Steve's original proposal of getting a new $1,500,000 mortgage on the commercial center. One million dollars of that mortgage would go to pay off Betsy's existing first, but the other half million would go directly to Betsy, equaling out the equity differences.

Equity $ 500,000
Plus cash   + 500,000 Excess from new loan on center
           $1,000,000 Betsy's equity

Second, there was the matter of enough cash to complete the deal. Half of the money needed to cash Betsy out had already been accounted for, from the excess of the new mortgage Steve would assume on the commercial center. The remaining half million was likewise easily obtained — from Bill. Bill had $250,000 to put down. And he was getting a new million-dollar mortgage on the apartment building. After paying off Steve's existing loan of $750,000, this would leave another $250,000, just the amount needed.

Cash
   $ 500,000 From new first on commercial center
      250,000 Cash down payment from Bill
   + 250,000 Excess from new mortgage on apartments (after
              paying off existing loan)
     $1,000,000 Cash available to Betsy

Values

Finally, there was the matter of the different prices between the two buildings. Mary. the agent, pointed out that prices were used to establish the value of the buildings. Once that was established, then as far as the investors were concerned, they only really had to be concerned about their equities. As long as they got their full equities out or transferred, it should make no difference to them what the prices on the two investments were.

Now that all the elements were there, the real problem, Mary pointed out, was to make everything work. It was a bit like taking a random deck of cards, throwing them up in the air, and having them all come down neatly arranged into order and suits. She began by explaining the exchange to Bill.

Bill was concerned about the entire deal. He simply wanted to buy the apartment building. He didn't care that Steve had a tax problem in the sale. Mary carefully pointed out that although there would be a few extra documents to sign, Bill would end up with the apartment building just as he wanted. She explained the deal to him in two stages.

First Stage of the Exchange for Bill

Bill would first buy Betsy's commercial center (see Figure 10-2). Since he had only $250,000 cash and the price was $2 million, he would get a million-and-a-half first mortgage and give Betsy a personal note for the balance. (The note would be for one day only and tied to the exchange escrow, but not secured by real property. We'll see how this note gets paid shortly.)

Bill was a bit shocked by the figures. He pointed out he didn't want to get a new first for that amount of money and he didn't see how he could pay off the one-day note for a quarter million dollars.

Mary said not to worry about the first, since Steve would quickly assume it. And Bill would have enough money to pay off the personal note before the deal was concluded. This left Bill perplexed. Then Mary explained the second stage of the exchange.

Second Stage of the Exchange for Bill

In the second stage (see Figure 10-3), Steve would trade $500,000 in equity in the apartment building for Bill's $500,000 in equity in the

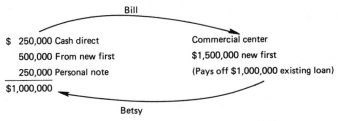

FIG. 10-2 First stage of exchange for Bill.

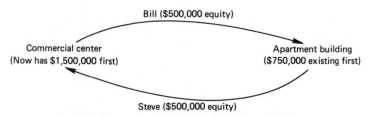

Bill ($500,000 equity)

Commercial center
(Now has $1,500,000 first)

Apartment building
($750,000 existing first)

Steve ($500,000 equity)

FIG. 10-3 Second stage of exchange for Bill.

commercial center. Steve would also assume the $1,500,000 new mortgage on the center, relieving Bill of all interest and liability there. Finally, Bill would refinance the apartment building, getting a new first mortgage of $1,000,000. From this amount (forgetting closing costs for this example) he would pay off the existing loan, leaving him just enough money to pay off his personal note to Betsy.

$ 750,000 Payoff on existing apartment building first
− 250,000 To pay off personal note to Betsy
$1,000,000 Received from new first on apartment building

Bill would end up with the apartment building and a $1 million loan on it. Since its price was $1,250,000, his equity would effectively be transferred into the equity of the building. And since he would be relieved of any liability on the loan on the commercial center and the personal note to Betsy would be paid, for all practical purposes the deal would be the same as if he simply bought the apartment building outright. Bill was satisfied.

Steve, who had been listening, however, was confused by the explanation. He wanted to know why Bill would get the new first mortgage on the commercial center when it was really he, Steve, who needed it. He said, "Bill's getting my mortgage for me on the commercial center?"

Mary brightened and said, "Precisely."

She went on to explain the financing. In order to balance out the exchange, Bill had to get the new mortgage on the commercial center. This allowed Betsy to receive half of her equity out in cash, and it gave Bill the $500,000 equity necessary to make the trade with Steve. Of course, in reality, since Bill would own the commercial center for only an instant before it was transferred to Steve, Steve would also have to qualify for the loan. The entire details of the transaction would have to be made known to the lender, else it would not work. (Most lenders will no longer allow assumption of mortgages without their specific approval.) The lender would have full knowledge and would understand that while the new first on the commercial center would initially be issued in Bill's name, Steve would assume it as soon as the transaction was completed (see Figure 10-4). Hence, Steve's credit and track record would also have to qualify.

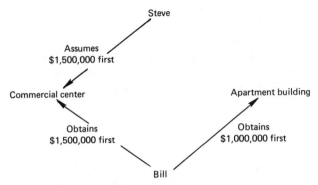

FIG. 10-4 Mortgages on the transaction.

Mary went on to point out that there was only one stage to the transaction for Steve (see Figure 10-5). He would simply trade his $500,000 equity in the apartment building for Bill's $500,000 equity in the commercial center, assuming the $1,500,000 first which had been obtained in Bill's name.

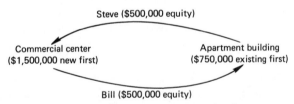

FIG. 10-5 One-stage transaction for Steve.

Steve's last question was to ask if it wouldn't be simpler to have Bill buy the apartment building directly from him. That would turn Steve's $500,000 equity into cash, and he could simply buy the commercial center directly from Betsy without going through all the rigmarole.

Mary answered that it certainly would be simpler. However, it wouldn't be a tax-free exchange. It would be a sale and subsequent purchase. In order to get tax-free status, there must be an *exchange* of properties. (And, prior to the *Starker* decision—see page 133—there can't be any time lapse between any two parts of the deal. The entire transaction has to happen simultaneously.)

Mary went on to explain that all the sales agreements, escrow, and attorney instructions would specify that one deal was contingent upon the other. There should be no chance that Bill could first buy the center and then refuse to trade Steve for the apartments. (The unity of time was also essential for the lender to go along and for Steve to get a tax-free exchange.) All deeds, mortgages, notes, and assumptions would be recorded simultaneously.

Finally, Mary carefully went over the exchange with Betsy. For her, it was the easiest explanation. She was simply selling her building to Bill for cash and a $250,000 personal note (see Figure 10-6).

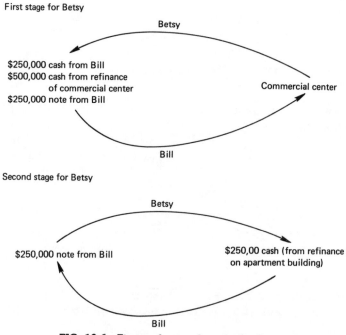

FIG. 10-6 First and second stages for Betsy.

Exchange for Betsy

	Commercial Center	
Received:	$250,000	From Bill in cash
	500,000	In cash from Bill's new first mortgage (which also paid off the existing $1 million first mortgage)
	250,000	Note from Bill

The note would bear no interest and would have a term of one day. As soon as the trade between Bill and Steve was completed, Steve would pay it off, thereby cashing out Betsy.

A diagram of the total transaction is shown in Figure 10-7. Betsy had only one concern. What if Bill refused to pay off the note once he had acquired the apartment building? Since it was unsecured, she might have difficulty collecting.

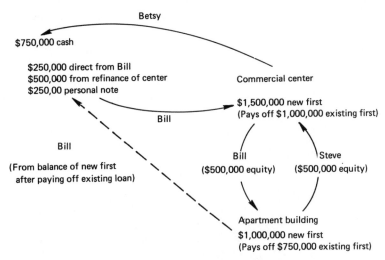

FIG. 10-7 Diagram of full exchange.

Mary pointed out that would not happen. The note was part of the exchange. Its payoff was linked, by the sales agreement and escrow instructions, to the entire transaction and would occur simultaneously with the recording of deeds. For practical purposes, there would be no time during which Bill owned the apartment building and had not paid off the note. All the financing would be arranged well before close of escrow. Betsy was satisfied.

The tax-free exchange enabled Steve to trade up without immediately paying any taxes on his gain. While the basic mechanics of tax-free exchanges are similar to our example, great variations are possible. Additionally, no two pieces of property and no two parties are going to be alike. Each buyer and seller will have his or her own specific tax situation and problems; each piece of property is unique, with its own values and financing. The reader, therefore, is cautioned against applying the previous fictional example to any real transaction without first checking out all parts of the transaction with an attorney familiar with tax-free exchanges.

TAX ANALYSIS OF THE EXCHANGE
EXAMPLE

Having gone through the mechanics of the exchange, now let's consider how it works from a tax viewpoint. While up to now we have been concerned with balancing equities, financing, and price, now we'll be concerned with basis, boot, and gain.

As we noted earlier, a great many of the problems involved in tax-free exchanges are caused by the fact that accountants, lawyers, and people who work with tax law look at property in a slightly different way from agents and investors who buy and sell it. An accountant might look at a piece of property as he or she looks at a dollar bill. When a taxpayer acquires a one-dollar bill, he or she has one dollar — it's that simple. An agent or investor looking at a piece of property, however, tends not to see it in the same way. In terms of a dollar bill, when an agent or investor acquires a dollar, it may equal only 20 cents. The other 80 cents is mortgaged.

While agents and investors talk about *equity* (the actual interest you have in a piece of property — its value *less* the mortgage on it), accountants tend to talk about *basis*. As we saw back in Chapter 8, the equity you have in a piece of property is of little consequence when taxes are being considered. What matters is what you paid less any depreciation and costs you may have deducted. The reason this leads to so much confusion in exchanges is that almost always equity (current sale price less mortgages) is different from basis. Let's review for a moment.

We have just described what equity is: price or value less mortgages. But there are two kinds of basis — original and adjusted. Original basis, you will recall, is the original price paid (or whatever other basis was originally used), less costs, when the property was acquired. Adjusted basis is the original basis *less* any reductions in it caused by depreciation. If we start with an original basis of $100,000 and over 10 years take $40,000 of depreciation, our adjusted basis is $60,000. Just as was the case in the original basis, it makes no difference what our leverage situation is. If we bought for $100,000 cash and then over the course of 10 years took out a $20,000 mortgage, paid it off, took out an $80,000 mortgage, and now have $50,000 left to pay, it in no way affects basis.

The market value of our property, after we've acquired it, also does not affect our basis. In the above example, if our property at the end of 10 years should now be worth $200,000 instead of the original price we paid of $100,000, our basis remains the same: $60,000.

Having made the distinction between equity and basis, we must now recall a further distinction—originally made in Chapter 7—between profit and gain. "Profit" is an agent's or investor's term that has to do with the amount of money you make on a transaction. For example, if you buy a building for $100,000 and sell it for $120,000 (forgetting costs for the moment), your profit is simple to figure — it's the difference, or $20,000.

"Gain," on the other hand, is a tax term, and it is not quite so simple to figure. In addition to the selling price, we also need to know the adjusted basis in order to figure the gain. The adjusted basis is the original basis (in this case the price less costs) less any depreciation. If you purchase the building, hold it for 10 years, and depreciate $40,000 of its value, your adjusted basis (again forgetting about costs of sale) is $60,000. Your gain, as shown in Table 10-1, is $60,000.

TABLE 10-1

Figuring gain		Figuring profit	
Original basis	$100,000	Sale price	$120,000
Less depreciation	– 40,000	Purchase price	–100,000
Adjusted basis	$ 60,000	Profit	$ 20,000
Sale price	$120,000		
Less adjusted basis	– 60,000		
Gain	$ 60,000		

The reason these calculations are critical, of course, is that you pay tax on gain, not profit.

Having thus recalled what gain and basis are, let us consider one last term, which was introduced in Chapter 9: "boot." You will recall that boot in a tax-free exchange is any nonqualifying property. In the case of a real estate exchange, any personalty is nonqualifying. This means that cash, personal property such as a boat or a car, or other personal items are boot. You will also recall that any mortgage you are relieved of is similarly called boot. This means that if you have a $100,000 piece of property with a $50,000 mortgage and you trade for another piece of property and during the course of the trade your mortgage is paid off, you've just acquired $50,000 (the mortgage value) in boot.

Now, let us go back to the commercial center that Stephen purchased. We'll consider the tax consequences of the transaction separately for each participant. Exhibit 10-2 shows the financial status of each of the three parties prior to the transaction.

EXHIBIT 10-2

Betsy's commercial center
Price	$2,000,000
Mortgage (existing)	1,000,000
Basis (original price less depreciation and costs)	800,000

Steve's apartment building
Price	$1,250,000
Mortgage (existing)	750,000
Basis	700,000

Bill
Cash	$ 250,000

Let us begin by considering the exchange from Betsy's point of view—first, her gain. (For this problem we are continuing to assume no closing costs.) Betsy's current basis is $800,000 and her sale price is $2 million, and so her gain on the transaction is $1,200,000.

Price	$2,000,000
Less basis	− 800,000
Gain	$1,200,000

It is worth repeating that as is often the case, Betsy's gain is considerably more than her equity in the property. Her equity, you will recall, was only $1,000,000.

Now, let us figure Betsy's boot (see Exhibit 10-3). We said that all cash in a real estate transaction was boot. Betsy received $250,000 in cash directly from Bill. She also received another $500,000 in cash when Bill refinanced the old mortgage on the commercial center. We also said that any personalty is boot. Consequently, the $250,000 personal note that Bill gave her counts in this group. Finally, we noted that any mortgage relieved is boot. Betsy had her $1,000,000 existing mortgage paid off when Bill purchased her property.

EXHIBIT 10-3 *Betsy's boot in the transaction*

Cash directly from Bill	$ 250,000
Cash converted from equity when Bill refinanced	500,000
Personal note from Bill	250,000
Mortgage relieved	1,000,000
TOTAL BOOT	$2,000,000!

Betsy's total boot is $2,000,000—the total value of her property. Does this mean that she must pay tax on the total amount? No. You will recall that we said that gain realized was recognized to the extent of boot received. Betsy's gain is $1,200,000. Since the boot is greater than the gain, the total gain is recognized. But that still leaves $800,000 in boot. What is to be done with it?

Total boot	$2,000,000
Gain recognized (taxable)	−1,200,000
Excess boot	$ 800,000

When there is more boot than gain realized, the excess boot reduces the basis of the original property.

In Betsy's case, the $800,000 in excess boot offsets the current basis she had in the commercial center. Since her current basis, you will recall, was $800,000, her new basis becomes zero. This is only natural, of course, since she has sold the building.

Reducing the basis to zero may seem simple-minded when related to Betsy, but we'll see its important implications when we come to Bill.

Betsy now must pay tax (either ordinary or capital gains, depending on her holding period) on a gain of $1,200,000. This is exactly the same amount she would have had to pay tax on if she had had a simple cash sale. Steve was correct when he assured her she had nothing to lose by going through with the exchange. (Of course, had she instead disposed of the property on an installment sale, she might have done considerably better. See Chapter 15.)

Bill Sherman also had tax consequences from the exchange. He was concerned that "with all the monkeying around you're doing with the properties, I don't want to end up with a tax bill as a buyer!"

Here's how his tax picture looked. Bill began by buying the commercial center for $2,000,000. Since it was a straightforward cash purchase, there was no gain or boot to him, and his basis became the purchase price less any costs (which we're not considering for this example). While the purchase was simple enough, taxwise, the sale was a bit more complicated. Bill traded his $2,000,000 commercial center for a $1,250,000 apartment building. Were there any dire consequences for him from this trade?

First, let us consider the gain on the sale of the commercial center. Bill's basis was $2,000,000 (his purchase price). His sale price was $2,000,000. There was obviously no gain.

Purchase price	$2,000,000
Sales price	−2,000,000
GAIN	$ 0

What about boot? Bill had an existing mortgage of $1,500,000 on the property (this is the new mortgage he obtained on purchase). He was relieved of this debt when Steve exchanged properties with him and assumed it. Bill, on the other hand, assumed Steve's old mortgage of $750,000.

Boot consists of mortgage relieved less mortgages assumed.

Mortgage relieved (on center)	$1,500,000
Mortgage assumed (on apartments)	− 750,000
BOOT	$ 750,000

It turns out, shocking Bill, that he received $750,000 of boot on the sale. His dismay was short-lived, however, when he realized that even though he had boot, there was no tax to pay, since he realized no gain. Remember, gain realized is recognized to the extent of boot received. No gain realized, none recognized. But what about the excess boot? As we noted with Betsy, excess boot reduces basis. In this case the $750,000 of boot reduces Bill's basis in the commercial center.

Basis of commercial center	$2,000,000
Boot received (excess)	− 750,000
NEW BASIS	$1,250,000

The new basis is transferred to the property Bill received in trade. Bill's basis in the apartment building now becomes $1,250,000. Since this is the price he originally intended to pay for it, it is easy to see that he came out all right on the deal. (It is necessary to transfer basis from the old property to the new in this fashion, rather than simply to take the purchase price of the new property, because in some cases purchase prices are manipulated in order to satisfy the egos of buyers and sellers.)

Finally, we come to Steve's tax consequences. Was there gain on the transaction?

Steve's basis in the apartment building was $700,000. His sale price was $1,250,000. The gain was obviously $550,000. (Note: We are using a shorthand method of calculation here. The IRS prefers a more technical calculation, explained in Chapter 13. The result, however, is the same either way for this example.)

Sale price	$1,250,000
Less basis	− 700,000
GAIN	$ 550,000

Steve realized a gain of $550,000. The question is now, How much of this gain will be recognized? All the rules we learned in the last chapter must be carefully considered (plus a couple of new ones we'll come to shortly). If the property qualifies, if Steve is not a dealer in real estate, and so on, the critical question is, How much boot is there for Steve? The gain realized will be recognized to the extent of boot received.

There is no boot for Steve! No cash passed through his hands. It was all handled between Bill and Betsy. The mortgage Steve assumed ($1,500,000) was twice the size of the one in which he was relieved, and so there could be no mortgage boot. Consequently, all the gain realized by Steve is nonrecognized and deferred to a future date. It is handled by reducing the basis on his *new property*. Instead of starting with a basis of the purchase price ($2,000,000), Steve begins with a reduced basis. (We'll look at the IRS formula for calculating this in Chapter 13.)

Purchase price	$2,000,000
Less nonrecognized gain	− 550,000
Beginning basis on center	$1,450,000

His basis in the commercial center begins at $1,450,000. That this does truly defer (and not cancel) the gain can be seen by the fact that if Steve were to turn around and sell the building for cash the next day for the same price he paid ($2,000,000), he would show an immediate gain of $550,000.

There are two critical rules involved in a tax-free exchange that we have thus far skimmed over and that now deserve to be emphasized.

In order to maintain the totally tax-free status of the taxpayer, it is necessary that the exchange part of the transaction be kept separate from any cash part.

In our example, Steve was relieved of any involvement in the cash transaction because Betsy and Bill handled all the cash. In real estate taxation terms, exchanges which keep the trade totally separate from the cash are called "clean" trades. Those that mix cash and trade are referred to as "dirty." Clean exchanges are usually easier to handle from a tax viewpoint, and there is usually much less chance they will be questioned by the IRS.

Generally, all parts of the transaction must close simultaneously in order to maintain tax-free status, but not always.

Normally all parts of the exchange must close simultaneously in order for the taxpayer to achieve tax-free status. However, in August 1979 a decision, in the case of *T. J. Starker v. the United States of America,* handed down in the Ninth Circuit Court of Appeals opened the door for possible deals involving delayed exchanges. The actual effect of this new ruling on other tax-free exchanges remains to be seen. Readers are cautioned to seek professional advice on the status of delayed or open exchanges before considering the use of them.

Obviously, not all tax-free exchanges will occur similarly to the one described here. In fact, each exchange, as we noted earlier, is different and must be treated uniquely. But this example should serve to illustrate the basic trade. In Chapters 11 and 12, we'll go into several of the consequences of handling an exchange such as this in a slightly different manner.

The type of exchange we have been considering thus far involves a purchase and sale first and then an exchange later. This is sometimes called "Alderson exchange." We'll refer to it as a "Type I" exchange (see Figure 10-8).

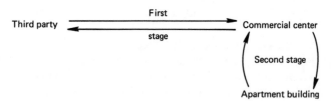

FIG. 10-8 Type I exchange.

There is another type of exchange equally acceptable, sometimes called a "Baird Publishing Company exchange," that involves having the exchange first and the purchase and sale second. We'll refer to it as a "Type II" exchange (see Figure 10-9).

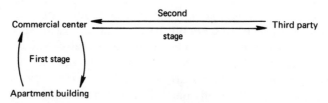

FIG. 10-9 Type II exchange.

In the first stage of the Type II exchange, Steve and Betsy simply trade their properties. Betsy assumes Steve's existing first mortgage and he assumes a new $1,500,000 mortgage on her property. The proceeds from this new mortgage go to pay off the existing $1,000,000 first, giving Betsy $500,000 in cash (see Figure 10-10).

In this first stage of the transaction, Steve gets the commercial center

FIG. 10-10 First stage of Type II exchange.

in trade for his equity and a new first mortgage. Betsy gets $500,000 in cash and a $500,000 equity in the apartment building. She now sells the apartment building to Bill on a cash basis. (Selling on a cash basis is all right for her, since she wants to "cash out" anyway.) From Bill she receives $250,000 in cash and another $250,000 when he gets a new first.

Bill's Purchase

$ 250,000	Cash
1,000,000	First
$ 750,000	Pays off existing first
250,000	To Betsy

Several things should be immediately apparent from this transaction. First, depending on the circumstances, it can be simpler than the Type I exchange we just went through. Second, the tax consequences, if the deal is handled properly, can be essentially the same as in the other type of trade. It is a useful exchange and, when conditions warrant, well worth considering.

The holding period for capital gains continues through a tax-free exchange.

Steve owned the apartment building for 5 years prior to the exchange. His capital gains holding period was 5 years. When he exchanges tax-free for the commercial center, his holding period transfers to the new property. After the exchange, his holding period on the commercial center is immediately 5 years. Were he to sell after one day, or instantaneously (as was the case with Betsy), the holding period would follow him. He would not lose his right to capital gains status on any recognized gain simply because he had traded properties.

The same holds true for Betsy in our second type of exchange. If she is otherwise entitled to capital gains treatment on her gain, she does not lose this right simply because she has exchanged the property tax-free. The holding period follows her through the trade.

11

Traps in the Tax-Free Exchange

THE BOOT TRAP

In Steve's trade, which we've been discussing, it is unlikely that there could be a problem with boot for Steve, since he is transferring his entire equity in the apartment building into the commercial center and handling no cash. If, however, he decided to transfer not all but only a part of his equity, a problem could arise. Let us say, for example, that Steve decided he wanted $100,000 of his equity out of the deal in cash. He intended transferring only $400,000 in equity to the new building.

One incorrect way of handling the deal is shown in Figure 11-1. The third party still would be used. However, when Bill buys the commercial center from Betsy, he assumes a new mortgage of $1,600,000—$100,000 more than in our earlier example. Everything else remains the same.

Bill's Purchase of the Commercial Center

Cash down	$ 250,000
New first	1,600,000
Note to Betsy	+ 250,000
	$2,100,000

Since the purchase price is only $2 million and the down payment, mortgage, and note add up to $2,100,000, Bill receives the excess $100,000 in cash himself. He doesn't hold on to it long, however.

When it's time to trade with Steve, we find that Bill's equity is short.

Steve's equity in apartments			**Bill's equity in center**	
$1,250,000	Price		$2,000,000	Price
− 750,000	First		−1,600,000	First
$ 500,000	Equity		$ 400,000	Equity

Bill makes up for his $100,000 equity deficiency by handing over to Steve the $100,000 in cash he receives when he buys the commercial center from Betsy. Steve pockets $100,000 in cash.

FIG. 11-1

The error should be clear, but just in case it isn't, in this exchange, the tax considerations for Bill and Betsy work out the same as with the actual example used in Chapter 10. (You can prove this by calculating them yourself.)

For Steve, however, there is a problem. He is getting $100,000 in cash, and *any cash received is boot*. That means that $100,000 of his $550,000 gain will be recognized (the rest, of course, will reduce his basis in the new property) and he'll have to pay tax on it (see Figure 11-2).

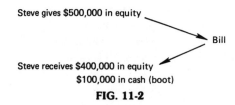

FIG. 11-2

While this boot error may seem obvious, thousands of agents and investors have made it. Yet, it is not at all necessary for Steve to get boot in this deal in order to get his $100,000 out in cash. The correct answer is easier than the incorrect one. He simply refinances before the exchange.

Let us consider the first stage of the transaction again. Bill buys the commercial center from Betsy:

Bill's Purchase of the Commercial Center

$ 250,000	Cash down
150,000	Note
+1,600,000	First mortgage
$2,000,000	

In this purchase Betsy receives the extra $100,000 instead of Bill, and the personal note is reduced by $100,000. That means that there is only $150,000 remaining to cash her out of the deal.

Steve proceeds differently from before. This time he obtains a new $100,000 second on his apartment building before the exchange. This is done outside the exchange escrow and totally separate from it.

Existing financing	$750,000
New second by Steve	+ 100,000
New financing before trade	$850,000

Steve has increased his indebtedness by $100,000 before the trade. Steve takes this $100,000 in cash (remember, we're not considering closing costs for this example) and pockets it. There are no tax considerations on a refinance. You will recall that change in the owner's indebtedness while owning property does not affect basis. Steve's basis in the property remains at $700,000.

Now the sale proceeds as before except that the exchange between Bill and Steve is of equities of $400,000, not $500,000 (see Figure 11-3). Once Bill acquires title on the apartment building, he goes ahead and refinances, getting the same $1,000,000 loan as before. However, now there is only $150,000 excess cash after the refinance.

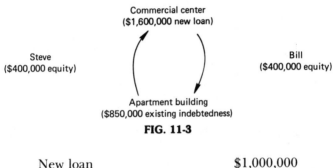

Commercial center
($1,600,000 new loan)

Steve
($400,000 equity)

Bill
($400,000 equity)

Apartment building
($850,000 existing indebtedness)

FIG. 11-3

New loan	$1,000,000
Existing loans to be paid off	– 850,000
Cash left over	$ 150,000

This $150,000 cash left over, however, is just the right amount of money to pay off the personal note given to Betsy. (Remember, the note was reduced by $100,000 when Bill refinanced the commercial center for that much more than in the earlier example.)

The reason for having Steve handle the refinance out of the exchange escrow and totally separate from it is to avoid any possibility that the money he received can be construed as boot.

Of course, there can be a problem if Steve refinances before the exchange. If Betsy or Bill decides not to go through with the deal, Steve will be left holding an extra $100,000 mortgage.

In theory, it should be possible for Steve to refinance as part of the entire exchange without allowing a time lapse between the two actions and still not have gain recognized. (After all, when refinancing is done, what difference does it make if the refinance is before another transaction or during as long as it's still a refinance?) The trouble with this is that any time a party claims tax-free status on an exchange and receives cash out of the deal, there is suspicion of boot. There might be arguments with the IRS over what that $100,000 really was, and the ruling might go against Steve. In the transaction, the risk of losing the deal after securing the $100,000 second would have to be balanced against the risk of having the $100,000 declared as boot.

It must be pointed out that no matter how the transaction is viewed, Steve does not get away without paying tax on the $100,000. If he refinances beforehand and has no boot problem, his new basis on the commercial center remains the same ($1,450,000). When he eventually sells for cash, he'll end up paying taxes on the $100,000 he receives now.

THE TITLE TRAP

There is a tendency to solve tax-free exchange dilemmas in a way more complicated than any we've discussed thus far, a way that involves changing the title.

In the actual method used in Chapter 10, the vehicle for allowing the exchange to take place was the personal note. This was a device to balance out Steve's $500,000 equity against Bill's $250,000 cash down payment. It is a good device and deserves to be used again. However, we have seen another method used for balancing a transaction that involves title transfer.

In this more complicated method, Bill does not buy Betsy's property outright. Rather, he buys only a *portion* of it. Bill gives Betsy his $250,000 cash and a note for $250,000 as before. In exchange, Betsy sells him half her equity in the commercial center (see Figure 11-4a). Now, together Betsy and Bill own the commercial center under a new title used to facilitate this transfer — as tenants in common. They refinance.

In the second stage of the transaction, Bill and Betsy trade their commercial center to Steve (see Figure 11-4b). Steve puts up his $500,000 equity in the apartment house and obtains another $500,000 from the refinance of the commercial center, thus paying off Betsy and Bill. At the end of the transaction, Bill refinances the apartment house, gaining another $250,000 to pay off Betsy's note as before (see Figure 11-4c). This type of exchange may be chosen to facilitate the financing. Steve gets his own loan, Bill his.

What has happened in this transaction is that Bill has transformed his $250,000 cash and $250,000 in a personal note into equity in the com-

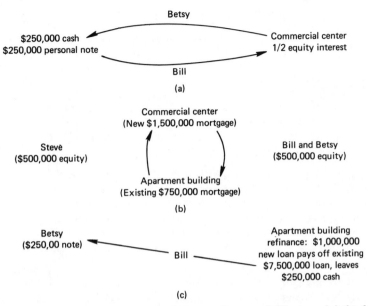

Betsy

$250,000 cash
$250,000 personal note

Commercial center
1/2 equity interest

Bill

(a)

Commercial center
(New $1,500,000 mortgage)

Steve
($500,000 equity)

Bill and Betsy
($500,000 equity)

Apartment building
(Existing $750,000 mortgage)

(b)

Betsy
($250,00 note)

Bill

Apartment building
refinance: $1,000,000
new loan pays off existing
$7,500,000 loan, leaves
$250,000 cash

(c)

FIG. 11-4 (*a*) First stage of title trap; (*b*) second stage of title trap; (*c*) third stage of title trap.

mercial center and then traded, along with Betsy, for Steve's apartment building. The gains for Betsy and Steve remain essentially the same. There is no boot in the deal, which is another reason why some prefer to use it. Steve's basis in the commercial center ends up the same. Finally, Betsy gets all cash out.

What, then is wrong with this method? Two things (beside the fact that the mortgage company that held the existing first on the commercial center probably would frown on the first stage of the transaction).

The first is simply its complexity. There can be tax and legal considerations in creating a tenancy in common, if only for a moment of time. And the difficulty in thoroughly explaining this method to investors such as Betsy and Bill can be overwhelming.

Second, this method might cost Steve his tax-free status on the exchange. Conceivably, it could be argued that Bill never really gained title to the commercial center, that title always remained with Betsy. The transfer of only part of the title might be seen as a subterfuge to conceal what is actually a cash purchase of the apartment building. Consequently, that portion of the exchange which involved Bill might be considered money received by Steve and indirectly paid to Betsy, or boot. And the tax consequences of this are obvious.

The solution to these potential problems is not to confuse the title in an exchange. If Betsy owns the property before the exchange, let her convey directly and totally to Bill and then Bill directly and totally to Steve. A lot of complexity and possible dire tax consequences may be avoided.

THE OPTION TRAP

Occasionally a situation will arise which will be different from any that we've considered thus far. In this case the motivating force in the transaction is an agent or investor who wants to buy a piece of property owned by a person we'll call the taxpayer. The taxpayer is reluctant to sell for cash but instead hopes to be able to arrange a suitable exchange. The agent or investor has only cash and so now a third party must be found in order to arrange a three-cornered exchange in which the agent or investor receives the taxpayer's property, the taxpayer trades with the third party, and the third party receives cash.

Frequently there is some doubt on the part of the taxpayer whether the agent or investor can come up with a suitable piece of property for which he or she can trade. Consequently, the taxpayer is reluctant to tie up his or her property in a sales contract. The solution is often the *option*. The agent or investor takes an option on the taxpayer's property in which the agreement is that if no suitable third party can be found within a specified period of time, the taxpayer will agree to sell the property to the agent or investor for cash.

There is nothing in particular wrong with this as long as either a three-cornered exchange occurs *before* the option runs out or a cash sale occurs after. If, however, a tax-free exchange occurs *after* the option runs out, the tax-free status of the exchange may be denied on the grounds that the taxpayer is entitled to cash for the property under the terms of the option and the agent or investor is obligated to pay it. An exchange after the option has expired would be presumed to be in consideration of money, and there might be no tax-free status.

The solution to this problem is simply stated. Care should be taken that all portions of the exchange are completed *prior* to the expiration of the option.

THE "STEP-SALE" TRAP

As we have said, care should be taken to see that all parts of the transaction occur simultaneously. In addition, care should also be taken that there are no steps within a sale. A step is one part of a large overall sale. Some exchanges have several steps, one occurring after the other, all contributing to a larger, overall transaction. Frequently these steps involve parts of the transaction conducted outside the exchange escrow. In fact, they may involve as many as half a dozen other escrows or more.

Exchanges which are step-sales can be recognized by the fact that the purpose of the overall transaction is to circumvent the paying of taxes immediately in what amounts to a cash sale. In other words, the exchange is merely one step in a larger transaction which avoids the payment of tax by trying to get the taxable gain deferred.

The government has recently denied tax-free status to many step-sales.

THE RECAPTURE TRAP

In a regular sale, as we saw in Chapter 7, recapture of depreciation may affect whether gain is taxed as ordinary income or as capital gains. In a tax-free exchange, however, some of the recaptured depreciation may result in increased gain realized. The rules for determining this are complicated and are best handled by a competent accountant or attorney.

These are some of the most common traps we have seen come up with tax-free exchanges. That does not mean that there aren't more or that there aren't variations of these. There are as many traps as the mind can conceive deals. The best solution, especially for those who haven't handled a tax-free exchange in the past, is to have someone, such as a tax attorney or CPA, carefully check over all the calculations before the deal goes too far. The short amount of time and the relatively small amount of money spent in this way can save a lot of trouble later on.

12

The Agent's or
Four-Cornered Exchange

The tax-free exchange may be limited in participants only by the imagination of the person putting it together. We have seen how three-cornered exchanges operate; now let us concentrate on exchanges with four or more parties. The four-cornered exchange tends to be different in a significant way from those we've considered thus far. While a three-cornered exchange is frequently initiated by a taxpayer who wishes to avoid immediately paying tax on a gain from a sale, a four-cornered exchange is most frequently arranged by an agent in order to solve a trading problem. It differs in that the agent often participates directly in the exchange—he or she *is* the fourth party — which is why this type of exchange is sometimes called an "agent's exchange."

The easiest four-cornered exchange to understand is a variation of the three-cornered exchange we have been discussing in the last few chapters. In this four-party exchange, an additional sale or purchase is added to the three-party exchange, as shown in Figure 12-1.

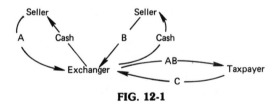

FIG. 12-1

In this simple four-cornered exchange, the parties are labeled seller, exchanger, and taxpayer. The sellers are simply those participants who sell their properties for cash to a participant, whom we shall call the exchanger, who arranges the transaction. In a three-cornered exchange (such as those we've seen in earlier chapters), the exchanger purchases one piece of property from one seller. In this simple four-cornered exchange, the exchanger purchases two pieces of property, A and B, from two sellers and then trades them with the taxpayer for C. The taxpayer is so labeled because it is he or she who always gets tax-free status on the transaction. In this transaction, both sellers show a recognized gain (unless, of course, they sell for a loss). The exchanger might or might not show recognized gain, depending on whether or not there is boot on the deal from the taxpayer.

A variation of this four-cornered exchange involves a buyer and a seller. In this variation, the exchanger buys a piece of property, A, from a seller, then trades A with the taxpayer for another piece of property, B, and then sells B to a buyer (see Figure 12-2).

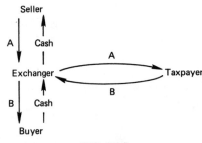

FIG. 12-2

In this case, the seller and the exchanger are liable to have recognized gain, since in both cases there is a cash sale involved. The deal still remains tax-free for the taxpayer unless there is boot involved.

It should be carefully noted in all these exchanges that the exchange portion of the transaction is handled separately from the purchase-sale portion. There are, as we noted earlier, two (or three) separate escrows. This is a critical aspect of the exchange if the taxpayer is to retain tax-free status.

In this last exchange it is interesting to note that the exchanger ends up not with property but with cash. Presumably, his or her motive in the transaction is to make a profit from the different values of the properties involved. This is just one step away from the most common type of four-cornered exchange — one in which the agent participates.

THE FOUR-CORNERED AGENT'S EXCHANGE

A four-cornered agent's exchange usually occurs when an agent is trying to put together a deal that cannot be otherwise completed. Frequently it is the case that the exchanger (from our last examples), for one reason or another, refuses to be the middle-person to the exchange. In such a case the agent may step in (at least temporarily) and be the fourth participant. This type of exchange is different from the other four-cornered exchanges we've thus far seen in that the agent is not a true principal but is acting for a client in a fiduciary relationship.

To understand the four-cornered agent's exchange, it is helpful to reconsider the two types of exchanges we discussed in Chapter 10. You will recall that in the one case (Type I) the purchase-sale took place in the first stage and the exchange in the second. In the other case (Type II) the exchange takes place first and the purchase-sale second.

THE TYPE I EXCHANGE
A Type I exchange is probably the most popular. It looks like Figure 12-3 in a four-cornered version.

FIG. 12-3   Type I exchange in a four-cornered version.

In this exchange, the agent typically represents the buyer of the taxpayer's property A. The agent, using the buyer's money, first purchases property B from the seller for cash. Then the agent trades property B for property A with the taxpayer. Eventually the agent conveys property A to the client.

This type of exchange occurs when the agent has a client who wants to buy a piece of property from a taxpayer for cash but for one reason or another (frequently a desire to avoid immediately paying tax on gain) the taxpayer does not want to sell for cash but instead wants to exchange. The agent now has to find a seller with a piece of property acceptable to the taxpayer. The agent buys the seller's property for cash and trades it with the taxpayer for the desired property, which the agent now can sell to the client for cash.

If the exchange is handled properly, usually the only person who has recognized gain is the seller (who always intended to sell his or her property for cash). The taxpayer achieves tax-free status because of the trade (if we assume no boot), and the agent receives no gain on the transaction. (The client, of course, has no gain because for him or her it is strictly a purchase.) The ultimate result for the agent is usually two commissions instead of one.

This type of exchange involves a sale first, then an exchange, and ultimately a purchase by the client. As we've noted before, it is extremely important that the *exchange* be handled separately from the *purchase-sale*. Any confusion of the two could result in loss of tax-free status for the taxpayer. (It goes without saying, of course, that both stages of the transaction must close simultaneously—see Starker, page 133.) There are other problems which arise in this type of exchange, but we'll wait to discuss them until we've had a chance to look at Type II.

THE TYPE II EXCHANGE

The difference between a Type II exchange and the one we've just considered is that in a Type II the exchange occurs first and the purchase-sale second (see Figure 12-4).

FIG. 12-4   Type II exchange in a four-cornered version.

In a Type II exchange, the agent typically represents the taxpayer, instead of the buyer as in Type I. The agent's client wants to dispose of his or her property but does not want the consequences of a cash sale. When a tax-free exchange seems the solution, the agent must find a suitable piece of property, property B in our example. The agent acquires title to property B, and the first stage is an exchange of property B with the taxpayer-client for property A. The second stage is a sale of property A to a buyer for cash. The cash ends up with the seller of property B.

In most cases, the need for the agent to participate in the transaction comes because, for a variety of reasons, the buyer does not want to be directly involved in a tax-free exchange. The agent thus steps in and acts as a principal.

The great danger with both types of agent's four-cornered exchanges is that the taxpayer will become directly involved in the purchase-sale portion of the transaction. If the taxpayer should become so involved, the exchange could lose its tax-free status.

This problem exists because of the dual role of the agent in the exchange. Although in theory the agent is acting only for a fiduciary, on the surface the agent's actions are those of a principal. Upon an examination of the transaction, the IRS may hold that regardless of the intent of the parties, the agent in both types was the agent of the taxpayer for the sole purpose of selling property A to the buyer for cash, that the exchange was a sham and a straight cash sale was what really occurred. In this case no tax-free exchange status will be given to the taxpayer. (The IRS is somewhat supported in this contention by the practice of real estate agents of finding buyers for sellers. Almost never do we hear of agents finding sellers for buyers.)

The way to reduce the possibility of such a claim by the government is to make it perfectly clear whom the agent is working for and also to show that the taxpayer does not in any way participate in any portion of the transaction other than the exchange. One method of accomplishing this is to use two title companies (if these are handling the escrows, or attorneys, if *they* are the escrow agents), one for each escrow; and even better, to use the title companies themselves as the agents instead of the real estate broker. In this circumstance, the taxpayer would have one title company handling the exchange and acting as his or her agent and the buyer would have another title company as an agent handling the other escrow. The result, at least for a moment in time, would be a five-cornered exchange. There would be a buyer, a seller, a taxpayer, and two title company-agents. The real estate broker would have stepped out of the transaction.

There would also, of course, have to be an agreement between the title companies to handle the transactions simultaneously. In addition, all documents would have to be kept separate and be given only to the escrow to which they were related. And each person would participate only in that escrow to which he or she was a principal party. The real estate broker would still be paid a commission, out of whichever escrow was appropriate, as long as the sales contract and escrow instructions provided for it.

Although the overall strategy of the four-cornered exchange is fairly simple (a rereading may help to simplify it), the handling of documents and escrows is a sophisticated operation. It is suggested that no agent try such an exchange without the aid of an attorney.

13

The Technical Treatment
of a Tax-Free Exchange

The calculation of boot, gain, and basis can be done by the convenient shorthand methods we have used thus far, or it can be done by using the precise methods preferred by the IRS. These methods have been adopted to give accurate answers in all circumstances. Since the IRS is the agency for whom all our calculations are made, it is wise to understand how it views them. In actual practice, however, an agent or investor should consult with a CPA or tax attorney before using them.

Let us begin by considering boot. We have mentioned that boot is both cash and personalty. We have had numerous examples in which boot was cash, but none in which it was personalty. Let us see how boot is treated, from the IRS viewpoint, when it is personalty.

We'll begin by reviewing boot treated as cash only.

BOOT AS CASH

John recently bought an apartment building for $260,000 cash. He has had it only a few years, and so he has depreciated it very little. Its current basis is $250,000. Now, John exchanges his apartment building with Helen for a large improved lot, which he intends to hold for investment. The lot has a fair market value of $240,000. To make the deal, Helen gives John $20,000 in boot.

Value of John's building	$260,000
Value of Helen's lot	$240,000
Boot given by Helen to John	+ 20,000
	$260,000

As any agent or investor will tell you, it's a fair trade, with neither side making any profit. Now let us figure the tax angle.

Value of Helen's boot and lot	$260,000
Current basis of John's building	−250,000
Gain	$ 10,000

The gain on the transaction for John is $10,000. At this point we must recall our discussion concerning gain realized and gain recognized. John has just realized a gain of $10,000. But, because this is a like-kind trade of qualified properties, is that gain recognized? Does he have to pay tax on it?

You will recall in our earlier discussion that there is no tax to be paid on property exchanged solely for other property. But where there is gain and where there is also boot, the gain realized is recognized to the extent of the boot received.

The boot was $20,000, but the gain realized was only $10,000. Since all of gain realized is recognized up to the amount of boot, the full gain of $10,000 is recognized.

Boot	$20,000
Less gain	−10,000
Recognized gain	$10,000

John would have to pay capital gains tax on the $10,000.

At this point, an inquisitive reader might ask, What happens to the other $10,000 of boot that was not recognized? The answer is that it is subtracted from the current basis of John's apartment building, reducing it from $250,000 to $240,000, and this now becomes the new or original basis of the lot he has purchased from Helen.

Current basis of apartment building	$250,000
Less boot not recognized	− 10,000
Original basis for new lot	$240,000

This is important because it illustrates that John hasn't avoided paying the tax on the second $10,000 of boot but has only put off payment until he eventually sells the lot. And herein lies a basic rule of tax-free exchanges.

In a tax-free exchange, the tax is not forgiven, but it is only deferred until a later date.

BOOT AS PERSONALTY

Jane, who is not a dealer in real estate, has a lot she purchased years ago for investment. Its current *basis* is $20,000, although its market value is $22,500. Jane now trades her lot to Sarah for another lot which has a fair market value of $19,000. To make the deal Sarah throws in an old Pontiac with a fair market value of $1,500 and $2,000 in cash.

Sarah's lot	$19,000
Sarah's Pontiac	1,500
Sarah's cash	2,000
	$22,500
Jane's lot	$22,500 (market value)

As can be seen, it is an even exchange. However, remember, Jane's lot has a basis of $20,000. That means that Jane will show a gain realized on the sale of $2,500.

Sarah's property	$22,500
Jane's basis	−20,000
	$ 2,500

The question is, What portion of this gain realized is recognized or taxable? The answer is all of it. Cash, of course, is considered boot. And anytime personalty (in this case, the car) is traded for realty, the personalty is also considered boot. There is $3,500 of boot in this deal (the car plus cash). Since the gain is $2,500, that portion is recognized. The other $1,000 of boot reduces Sarah's basis on the new lot (see Figure 13-1).

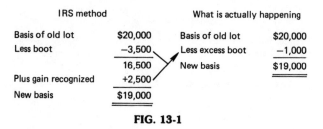

FIG. 13-1

CALCULATING BOOT, BASIS, AND GAIN BY THE IRS METHOD

The basic formulas for boot, basis, and gain are as follows:

BOOT = cash + personalty − liability assumed + liability relieved

REALIZED GAIN = value of property received + cash (personalty) + liability relieved − adjusted basis of property given − liability assumed

BASIS OF NEW PROPERTY = old basis + liability assumed + − cash (personalty) − liability relieved + gain recognized

An additional formula which may prove useful is for calculating recognized gain.

RECOGNIZED GAIN = boot (up to the extent of gain realized)

These formulas are fairly simple, though at first glance they may seem complex. Perhaps the best way to familiarize oneself with them is by using them in various examples. It is suggested that the reader refer back to these formulas when following the calculations for the rest of this chapter.

Let us begin by using the method to figure boot, gain, and basis on a simple exchange. Sloan has an apartment building with a value of $1.7 million and an adjusted basis of $1 million. Sloan eventually trades his apartment building to Harry, who assumes his mortgage and gives him in return another apartment building with a fair market value of $1,200,000 plus $200,000 in cash (see Figure 13-2).

What is Sloan's boot, his gain realized, and his gain recognized?

The boot is cash plus liability relieved (for Sloan, there is no personalty or liability assumed to be concerned with in this example).

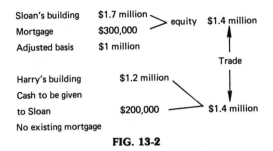

FIG. 13-2

Cash	$200,000
Liability relieved	+300,000
Boot	$500,000

Sloan's gain is figured in this fashion:

Value of Harry's building	$1,200,000
Plus cash	200,000
Plus mortgage on Sloan's building being assumed by Harry	+ 300,000
	$1,700,000
Less Sloan's adjusted basis on old building	−1,000,000
Sloan's gain *realized*	$ 700,000

Of the gain realized ($700,000), the amount recognized is the amount of the boot up to the full gain realized. Since the boot is only $500,000, that is the amount recognized on which Sloan will have to pay taxes. The basis of the new apartment building for Sloan will be the adjusted basis of the old building less boot plus gain recognized. Since both boot and gain recognized are $500,000, the basis remains the same: $1 million.

Adjusted basis of old building	$1,000,000
Less boot	− 500,000
	$ 500,000
Plus gain recognized	+ 500,000
Basis of new building	$1,000,000

In addition to illustrating the IRS method, Sloan's example reaffirms that great care must be taken in an exchange when an assumption of mortgages takes place. Sloan received only $200,000 in cash, yet his taxable gain for the exchange is $500,000. Even if he has owned the building for over a year and can claim capital gains treatment, much of the *cash* will have to be paid in taxes.

This example was particularly onerous because Sloan had a mortgage on his properety while Harry didn't. In the case where both properties are mortgaged, *the mortgage the taxpayer is relieved of on his or her own property is offset by the mortgage he or she assumes on the property being traded.* For purposes of figuring boot, consider the case shown in Figure 13-3, where both properties are mortgaged.

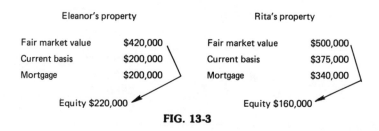

Eleanor's property		Rita's property	
Fair market value	$420,000	Fair market value	$500,000
Current basis	$200,000	Current basis	$375,000
Mortgage	$200,000	Mortgage	$340,000
Equity $220,000		Equity $160,000	

FIG. 13-3

Eleanor has $60,000 more equity in her property than Rita has in hers. To make the trade, Rita gives Eleanor $60,000 in cash. What is the total boot, the gain realized, the gain recognized, and the new basis for each of them?

Eleanor's Boot

Let us consider Eleanor's boot first. She has a $200,000 mortgage on her property, which Rita will assume. This gives Eleanor relief from the liability. However, Eleanor is going to assume an even bigger mortgage of $340,000 on Rita's property. In this case, Eleanor's mortgage from which she is relieved is totally offset by the even bigger mortgage she will assume on Rita's property. Consequently, there is no mortgage boot. The only boot, then, is the $60,000 in cash that Rita is giving. (The excess of the mortgage assumed over the mortgage released does not offset the cash received as boot.)

Eleanor's Gain

Eleanor's gain is $220,000 (see Exhibit 13-1). However, since only the cash, or $60,000, is treated as boot, only $60,000 of the $220,000 is *recognized* and taxable.

EXHIBIT 13-1

Value of Rita's property received	$500,000
Cash received	60,000
Liability relieved	200,000
Total consideration received	$760,000

EXHIBIT 13-1 (Cont.)

LESS:

Adjusted basis of Eleanor's property	$200,000	
Liability assumed on Rita's property	340,000	
		−$540,000
GAIN REALIZED		$220,000

Eleanor's Basis

The basis of Eleanor's new apartment building is shown in Exhibit 13-2.

EXHIBIT 13-2

Adjusted basis of old property		$200,000
Liability assumed on new property		+340,000
		$540,000
From this amount is subtracted:		
Cash received	$ 60,000	
Liability relieved on old property	200,000	
		−260,000
		$280,000
Finally, the amount of gain is added:		+$ 60,000
Basis of new property for Eleanor		$340,000

Rita's Boot

Now let us consider the deal from Rita's point of view. First, there is the matter of boot (see Exhibit 13-3). To calculate the boot we add the liabilities Rita is relieved of and subtract the boot she gave and the new mortgage she will assume.

EXHIBIT 13-3

Old mortgage relieved		$340,000
LESS:		
Boot given	$ 60,000	
New mortgage assumed	200,000	
		−260,000
BOOT		$ 80,000

Rita's Gain

The *gain* for Rita on the exchange is $125,000, as shown in Exhibit 13-4. However, since boot is only $80,000, only $80,000 of the $125,000 is *recognized* and taxable.

EXHIBIT 13-4

Value of property received	$420,000
Liability relieved on old property	+340,000
Total consideration	$760,000
LESS:	

Adjusted basis of property transferred	$375,000	
Cash paid	60,000	
Liability assumed	200,000	
		−635,000
GAIN REALIZED		$125,000

Rita's Basis

And, finally, Exhibit 13-5 shows the basis for Rita's new property.

EXHIBIT 13-5

Adjusted basis of old property	$375,000
Liability assumed	200,000
Cash paid	60,000
	$635,000
LESS	
Liability relieved	−340,000
	$295,000
PLUS	
Gain recognized	+ 80,000
Basis of new property	$375,000

At this stage, some readers may be making demands for simplicity. If the boot transferred is what the tax is paid upon, why does the IRS bother with all the intricate calculations? If a deal is going to have $60,000 in cash, why not simply say that the person receiving it will have to pay taxes on that amount?

There are several reasons against taking the simplistic approach. The basic reason, of course, is that the complicated method is the one preferred by the IRS. In addition, cash is not the only ingredient that goes into boot. As we have seen, any other personalty, such as a car, is also considered boot. And, what is far more important, any mortgage relief that is not offset by another mortgage assumed also goes into boot. Boot *is not* simply the cash traded in an exchange.

Second, if there is no gain on the sale, there is no tax to pay regardless of what the boot may be. In all the deals we have considered thus far, there has always been some gain, but it is not inconceivable that there could be no gain. Consider an extreme example: A property has a basis of $500,000 and is traded for a property worth $200,000 and $250,000 in cash. When we figure the gain by subtracting the value of the property and cash received from the basis of the old property, we find there is a loss:

New property	$200,000
Cash	250,000
	$450,000
LESS:	
Basis of old property	−500,000
LOSS	($ 50,000)

In this case, even though there is $250,000 of boot, there is no tax to pay, since the trade shows a loss. In order to know this, however, we first had to calculate the possible gain. To know tax payable we must know *both* boot and gain. (Note: Losses are not deductible in tax-free exchanges.)

14

Foreclosure and Loss

In a foreclosure, the outstanding balance on the mortgage at the time of foreclosure is considered the sale price. The gain or loss is calculated just as if there had been a regular sale.

page 162

The amount of the loss on the sale of a piece of investment property that can be applied toward ordinary income is severely restricted

page 163

Currently, the maximum amount that may be deducted from ordinary income as a loss is $3,000 per year.

page 164

Half of all long-term capital loss is not deductible. All allowable capital loss, however, may be carried forward into future years.

page 164

The easiest type of sale to understand is one for cash where a profit occurs. Sometimes, however, property is sold without profit, as at foreclosure sale. Other times there may be a loss on the sale. And at still other times it may be advantageous from a tax viewpoint not to have a cash sale, but to have instead an installment sale. Let us begin by considering what happens from a tax viewpoint when an investment property goes into foreclosure.

In a foreclosure, the outstanding balance on the mortgage at the time of foreclosure is considered the sale price. The gain or loss is calculated just as if there had been a regular sale.

In a foreclosure, if a property has been depreciated to a basis of $750,000 yet the remaining balance of the mortgage is $900,000, the basis is subtracted from the sale price (mortgage value at foreclosure), which in this example results in a gain of $150,000—even though the property has been lost through foreclosure and no money is received by the investors on the sale!

This is the great danger inherent in overleveraging property. Mortgage values tend to remain high, while depreciation reduces basis. When the property fails because of the overleveraging, the investors not only lose the investment, but may also be required to pay taxes on gain as well. To make matters worse, all or part of the depreciation taken under an accelerated method still must be taxed as ordinary income. At the time of the investment, however, many investors may not see this problem.

If in our example an investor or group of investors has invested $50,000 in a highly leveraged $950,000 investment property, the investors may not have been worried too much about foreclosure. If they anticipated receiving $200,000 in depreciation deductions before foreclosure, as they have, and they are in a 50 percent tax bracket, they may have believed that they would still come out all right. In their tax bracket, the tax saving on the loss may be interpreted as making a profit even on the foreclosure.

Depreciation loss received	$200,000
Tax bracket	× 0.50
Tax saving	$100,000
LESS:	
Investment loss	− 50,000
NET PROFIT	$ 50,000

After foreclosure, however, gain on the sale of the property must be calculated. If, as in our example, depreciation has lowered the basis to $750,000 and there remains $900,000 on the mortgage (the property was purchased for $950,000), the gain is $150,000. Without knowing exactly the method and term of depreciation, it is impossible to say what portion of the gain is due to accelerated depreciation and what portion to straight-line. If, however, we assume it is all straight-line (highly unlikely, though possible) the gain will be taxed at capital gains rates. Using the regular method, this means simply cutting it to 40 percent and adding it to ordinary income.

$$Gain\ \$150,000 \times 0.4 = 60,000$$

The investors now add $60,000 to their ordinary income, boosting their tax brackets and significantly lowering their return on the investment.

Of course, as we have said, it is unlikely that such a large amount of depreciation could be accumulated without the use of an accelerated depreciation method. If such an accelerated method were used and the amount due to acceleration were taxed at ordinary rates, it would dramatically increase the total tax owed and reduce even further the return on the investment.

Although in property which is overleveraged there can be gain in the event of foreclosure, in other properties where leveraging is normal, an actual loss may occur.

The amount of the loss on the sale of a piece of investment property that can be applied toward ordinary income is severely restricted.

It is important at this juncture that the reader have clear in his or her mind that we are now talking about a different type of loss from what we have discussed before. Prior to this point, we have been speaking of the loss that occurs each year as part of the *operation* of a piece of investment property. In this section we are speaking of the loss that occurs upon the *sale* of a piece of investment property. Deducting expenses from operations in real estate is unlimited. Deducting the loss on sale is severely limited.

If a piece of property is sold at a loss that is considered either long-term (held for one year or longer) or short-term, a certain portion of that loss may be deducted from ordinary income. (It should be carefully noted that all losses, whether long-term or short, must be offset by *all* gains from *all* assets, whether they be real estate, stocks, furniture, or something else, and only then if a net loss exists can it be deducted as indicated here. This, however, is a sophisticated procedure beyond the scope of this work and requires the work of an experienced accountant or tax lawyer.) The amount of loss that can be deducted from ordinary income has certain very specific limitations.

Currently, the maximum amount that may be deducted from ordinary income as a loss is $3,000 per year.

Before 1976 the maximum capital loss that could be deducted from ordinary income was $1,000. In 1977 it increased to $2,000, and in 1978 it became the current $3,000. This amount of money, however, may not simply be deducted as such from income.

Half of all long-term capital loss is not deductible. All allowable capital loss, however, may be carried forward into future years.

In figuring long-term capital loss, half the amount is immediately excluded. Then up to $3,000 a year may be deducted. Losses of $10,000 and $20,000 are treated as shown in Exhibit 14-1.

EXHIBIT 14-1 *Long-Term Capital Loss*		
Total loss 1978	$10,000	$20,000
Less ½ not deductible	− 5,000	−10,000
Deductible amount	$ 5,000	$10,000
Maximum deduction 1978	− 3,000	− 3,000
Balance to carry forward to 1979	$ 2,000	$ 7,000
Amount deducted 1979	− 2,000	− 3,000
Balance to carry forward to 1980	$ 0	$ 4,000
Amount deducted 1980		− 3,000
Balance to carry forward to 1981		$ 1,000
Amount deducted 1981		− 1,000
Balance to carry forward to 1982		$ 0

The one-half exclusion does not apply to short-term capital losses. A short-term capital loss can be deducted from ordinary income on the basis shown in Exhibit 14-2.

EXHIBIT 14-2 *Short-Term Capital Loss*	
Total loss 1978	$10,000
Deducted 1978	− 3,000
Balance to carry forward 1979	$ 7,000
Deducted 1979	− 3,000
Balance to carry forward 1980	$ 4,000
Deducted 1980	− 3,000
Balance to carry forward 1981	$ 1.000
Deducted 1981	− 1,000
	$ 0

15

The Ins and Outs of Installment Sales

Installment sales can be a very useful method of reducing the taxes on
the sale of real estate. If used properly, they can be an enormous boon
to the taxpayer and may even result in extra deals for the agent. If used
improperly, however, they may result in wasted effort and, in some cases,
in unexpected tax liability for the seller.

An installment sale, quite simply, spreads the taxable gain from the
sale of real estate over a period of years. This is quite different from
most real estate transactions, which tend to be cash sales. In the cash
sale, a buyer usually gives the seller a down payment and then takes out

a mortgage from a lender for the balance of the price. Out of the mortgage money, the seller receives the rest of the sale price, in cash. Consequently, for the seller the sale is totally cash, and tax must be paid on all gain in the year of the transaction.

On the other hand, if the seller were not to sell for cash but instead were to sell on the installment plan (and meet specific conditions), the tax on the gain from the sale would only need to be paid as it was received.

For example, let's assume that both the taxable gain and the profit on the sale of a piece of investment property are $20,000. In a cash sale, the tax on the entire $20,000 must be paid in the year received. If, however, the money were spread over 2 years in installments, then (if other conditions were met) only the amount received each year would need to be declared as taxable in that year.

The advantages of the installment plan should be obvious. Since we have a graduated income tax, the more money received in any one year, the higher the percentage of tax. If the gain came to the taxpayer entirely as ordinary income, it is most likely that the total tax on the $20,000 in one year (because of the higher bracket it would boost the taxpayer into) would be greater than the total tax payable on installments spread over 2 years. If the gain were spread over more years, the benefits could be even greater.

For taxpayers in higher income brackets, who may take advantage of capital gain on the sale of a piece of property, the installment plan still offers some advantage. If, in our last example, the taxable gain and profit were both $70,000, then on a cash sale the taxpayer would pay 40 percent as ordinary income (capital gains). Under an installment sale, as we shall see, the taxpayer could elect to take up to $21,000 the first year and the remainder in subsequent years (if specific conditions were met). The smaller amount now might be taxed in a lower tax bracket—a substantial saving over a cash sale. (For a further explanation of capital gains, check Chapter 7.)

RULES FOR INSTALLMENT
CONTRACT SALES

In order to qualify for an installment sale, the seller must receive no more than 30 percent of the selling price in the year of the sale.

The 30 percent figure is set in stone—it may not be violated. If the seller receives even a few dollars more than 30 percent, installment sale advantages may be disallowed by the IRS.

It has become common practice for many agents and investors to insist on 29 percent or 29½ percent down. Their reasoning is that sometimes it is difficult to calculate down to the last penny the total amount of money coming to the seller, prior to the close of escrow. If a 30 percent figure were used and the seller ultimately received, for example, 30.012 percent or some other figure above 30 percent, the installment advantages could be disallowed. The dictum followed here is "better safe than sorry."

The selling price includes cash, fair market value of other property, new notes to seller, and amortization of old notes.

The selling price is the total price paid by the buyer for the property. If the buyer assumes an existing first mortgage with a balance of $50,000, gives a car to the seller in trade with a fair market value of $10,000, puts in $20,000 in cash, and gives a second mortgage to the seller of $20,000, the selling price is $100,000.

First mortgage assumed	$ 50,000
New car to seller	10,000
Cash to seller	20,000
Second mortgage to seller	20,000
Selling price	$100,000

The 30 percent down payment is calculated on the basis of the selling price. Commissions and selling expenses do not reduce the sale price for calculating the down payment.

If Harry sold a piece of property for $100,000, paid a $6,000 commission, and had closing costs of $2,500, the maximum down payment he could receive and still qualify for an installment sale would be $30,000.

When *gain* is figured on the sale, the sale price is reduced by the commission and expenses—in this case down to $91,500. But for determination of the 30 percent rule on installment sales, the full sale price is used. (It should be noted, however, that dealers in real estate actually may deduct any such commissions and expenses as a direct business expense.)

Figuring gain				*Figuring maximum initial payment*	
Sale price		$100,000		Sale price used to determine 30% rule	$100,000
Commission	$6,000				
Selling expenses	2,500				
	− 8,500				
Adjusted sale price used to determine gain on sale		$ 91,500			

If a full 30 percent down payment is used, there may be no additional payments in the year of sale.

The total of all payments in the year of sale may not exceed 30 percent. One trap that agents and investors occasionally get into is to receive 30 percent down with a mortgage over, for example, 5 years for the balance. Payments on the mortgage may be set up on a monthly basis. If the seller receives the full 30 percent in the sale and then receives even one monthly payment on the mortgage balance in the same year (exclusive of interest), it puts that seller above a total of 30 percent in that year. This would, of course, result in the disallowance of an installment sale.

Payments must be made in two or more installments and must cover at least 2 years.

It is not necessary that any payment be made in the year of sale. It is necessary, however, that there be at least two payments and that they be spread out over at least 2 years. There is no maximum number of payments. It is possible to spread the payments out over 30 years or longer if desired.

A payment in the year of sale includes all cash or other property given to the seller. It does not include new mortgages given to the seller. It also does not include mortgages assumed by the buyer, unless the mortgage assumed is in excess of the seller's basis, in which case the excess is considered a payment in the year of sale.

Down payment in year of sale includes:

Cash
Other property given
Difference between seller's basis and existing mortgage (if mortgage is higher)

Down payment in year of sale does not include:

New mortgages
Assumed mortgages when lower than seller's basis

While it can clearly be seen that any cash or other property given to the seller is part of the down payment, it is not so easy to see what is meant by a mortgage assumed by the buyer in excess of the seller's basis. This area, in fact, is one of the great traps of the installment sale and accounts for a large portion of badly handled deals. Let's consider the problem.

You will recall that for tax purposes, we are constantly dealing with a taxpayer's basis in a piece of property. The current, or adjusted, basis is normally the original purchase price plus any costs of sale, minus any depreciation. *Basis is not affected by indebtedness.*

Henry buys a home for $47,000. His closing expenses come to $3,000, making his adjusted basis at the time of purchase $50,000. Since the home is his personal residence, Henry cannot depreciate it, and so there is no depreciation to lower basis. (Henry could, however, increase his basis by adding improvements to the property. Adding a swimming pool for $12,000 or a tennis court for $15,000 would add those sums to the basis. Henry makes no improvements, however, and so his basis remains at $50,000.)

When Henry bought the home, he obtained a first mortgage for $40,000. He owned the property for 5 years, during which time an enormous jump in the value of real estate took place. His home's value increased to $90,000. Henry, thinking he would liquidate some of the equity, took out a new first mortgage of $72,000, paying off the existing loan. While Henry's indebtedness shot up to $72,000 from the original $40,000, his basis did not change. It remained at $50,000 (see Exhibit 15-1).

EXHIBIT 15-1

		Basis
Original mortgage		$40,000
Down payment and closing costs		+10,000
Original purchase price		$50,000
New mortgage	$72,000	
New equity	+18,000	
New value of property	$90,000	

Now, Henry has decided to sell. His property has gone up even more since he refinanced, and so he is able to sell for $100,000. The buyer gives him $10,000 *cash* and a new mortgage for $18,000, with the *buyer assuming the existing first mortgage* of $72,000. Now, Henry has to answer the question, what are the total payments in the year of sale?

Existing mortgage	$ 72,000
Cash down	10,000
Second mortgage to Henry	18,000
Total price	$100,000

At first glance, it might seem that the total payments in the year of sale are $10,000. (You will recall that new mortgages do not count in determining the payments in the year of sale.) Since the existing loan is at $72,000, the only cash Henry supposedly receives is the buyer's down payment. Unfortunately, this method of calculating the down payment for installment sales is incorrect.

The down payment also includes the portion of a mortgage assumed by the buyer that is in excess of the seller's basis. Henry's basis has not changed since he bought the property 5 years earlier. It remains at $50,000.

Existing mortgage	$72,000
Basis	−50,000
Additional payment in year of sale	$22,000

The theory here is that Henry actually received the $22,000 difference between the new mortgage and the basis in cash when he refinanced. While, as we've said, a refinance does not have immediate tax consequences, it may catch up to the seller when it is time to dispose of the property. That $22,000 excess Henry received prior to the sale is all treated as part of the down payment in the year of sale and contributes to the total under the 30 percent rule.

This method of handling payments in the year of sale can be crucial when an installment sale is arranged. You will note in our example that if the excess money were not treated as a payment in the year of sale, Henry would be receiving only $10,000, well within the 30 percent limitation. But, by including the excess of mortgage over basis, Henry now receives $32,000, or over the limit allowed to qualify as an installment sale. Henry's claim for an installment sale would undoubtedly be denied by the IRS.

At one time, the refinancing by a taxpayer of a piece of property brought little worry with regard to installment sales, because property prices tended to remain fairly stable. But in recent years, with the rapid inflation in the price of real estate, many owners (particularly homeowners) have refinanced their properties, liquidating their increased equity. When it comes time to sell, if they intend to sell on an installment sale, they can be hit by this very problem. (Note that it makes no difference whether the buyer assumes the mortgage or takes the property subject to it—the rule still applies.)

The contract price is the total amount of all payments to be received by the seller.

The contract price is used to determine the percentage of each payment that will be taxable. Without knowing the contract price, it is impossible to determine the tax. It is very important to understand that the contract price is most often quite different from the sale price. In our last example, the contract price was $50,000, even though the selling price was $100,000. Let us see how.

The contract price means how much the seller is receiving on the sale, exclusive of the seller's indebtedness (except as noted above with regard to mortgage in excess of basis). It can be thought of as the total amount of all installments (exclusive of interest) that the *seller* will get.

Let us take an example. If we suppose that our friend Henry never refinanced his property, he would still have approximately a $40,000 mortgage on it. Now, if he sells for $100,000, his contract price will be the difference between his existing indebtedness and the selling price.

Selling price	$100,000
Mortgage	− 40,000
Contract price	$ 60,000

Note that when we calculate the contract price, it makes no difference whether the seller is receiving the money in the form of cash, personal property, or a new mortgage. The total of all monies to the seller in whatever form (exclusive of existing mortgages) constitutes the contract price.

However, our seller, Henry, as we noted earlier, did not keep his original mortgage. He refinanced and got a new loan for $72,000.

When the existing mortgage exceeds the basis, the excess is included as part of the contract price.

It is critical to understand that when the existing mortgage is *below* the basis, the contract price, as we've just seen, is the difference between the selling price and the mortgage. When the existing mortgage is higher than the basis, however, the contract price includes the difference between the selling price and the basis, as in our original example.

Excess of mortgage over basis	$22,000
Cash down	10,000
Second mortgage to seller	18,000
Contract price	$50,000

CALCULATING THE TAXABLE GAIN

The primary tax purpose of using an installment sale is to spread the payments on the sale of the property over several years in order to pay a lower tax than would be paid if only one payment were made. The tax itself is payable, as we've noted, in the year the installment is received. It is often the case, however, that only a portion of each installment is taxable—that portion that represents a gain on the sale. The other portion of the installment may merely represent a return on the taxpayer's investment. It is necessary to know what portion of each installment is taxable in order for a taxpayer to calculate the taxes to be paid on the sale in any given year, and thereby to determine what the advantages are of using the installment method.

The portion of each payment which is taxable is the percentage found by dividing the contract price into the gain.

The rule is actually quite simple. Consider an example. Let's suppose that our friend Henry has the same adjusted basis on his house as we discussed before, $50,000. Let us further suppose that in addition to the first loan of $40,000 he originally took out, he subsequently obtained a second mortgage from a lender for $10,000. At the time of sale, both his basis and indebtedness are the same, $50,000.

BASIS	$50,000
First mortgage	$40,000
Second mortgage	+10,000
Indebtedness	$50,000

Henry sells his house for $100,000 on the following terms. The buyer puts down $10,000 cash and gives Henry a third mortgage for $40,000 payable in four equal installments over the next 4 years. This gives him a contract price of $50,000.

Cash down	$10,000
Third mortgage	+40,000
Contract price	$50,000

Henry's gain on the property is determined by subtracting his adjusted basis ($50,000) from the selling price, which, after commission and other expenses have been deducted, comes to $100,000. (Note that for purposes of determining gain on the sale, commission and closing costs are first deducted from the selling price.) The gain is $50,000.

Selling price	$100,000
Basis	− 50,000
Gain	$ 50,000

The payment schedule is as follows:

Year	Payment	
Year of sale	$10,000	Down payment
2	10,000	
3	10,000	Third-mortgage
4	10,000	payments
5	10,000	

In order to find what portion of each payment is taxable, the gain is divided by the contract price:

$50,000 Gain ÷ $50,000 Contract price = 100%

In this example, 100 percent of each installment is taxable. The reader should carefully note that just because each installment is fully taxable does not mean that there has been no advantage to the installment sale. Without the installment sale, $50,000 would be fully taxable in the year of sale. With the installment plan, $10,000 is taxable each year for 5 years. Presumably, the tax on $10,000 a year is considerably less than the tax on $50,000 in one year.

Let us take another example. This time let's suppose that when Henry bought his house for $50,000, he put $25,000 down. As before, he sells for $100,000, only this time the buyer puts $25,000 down and gives Henry a second mortgage of $50,000 payable in five equal installments over 5 years ($10,000 a year).

Henry's contract price is the total of all cash, personal property, and new mortgages he receives. In this case it's $75,000.

Cash down	$25,000
Second mortgage	+50,000
Contract price	$75,000

Henry's gain on the sale is the same as in the last example. His basis is $50,000, the selling price is $100,000, and so the gain is $50,000.

Selling price	$100,000
Basis	− 50,000
Gain on sale	$ 50,000

The taxable portion of each payment (including the first) is the percentage found by dividing the contract price into the gain:

$$\$50,000 \text{ Gain} \div \$75,000 \text{ Contract price} = 66\frac{2}{3}\%$$

Two-thirds of each payment, including the first, is taxable. (The remainder is a return of the original capital invested.)

If there is any recaptured income under IRS Code Sections 1245 and 1250, it is reported *first* on the installment method.

You will recall that in Chapter 7 we discussed recapture of depreciation that may occur upon sale when an accelerated method of depreciation has been used. Occasionally, it will happen that in an installment sale part of the gain will be treated as capital gains and part, because of the recapture rules, will be treated as ordinary income. The question arises, Which portion of each payment will be taxed as capital gains and which portion taxed as ordinary income?

The answer is that *all ordinary income must be accounted for first.* Only after it has been completely accounted for can the remaining income be treated by the capital gains method.

Let us consider the case of Margaret. Margaret owned an apartment house which she bought for $150,000. During her period of ownership, she deducted $100,000 of depreciation. Of that amount, $50,000 came under the recapture rules.

Purchase price	$150,000	
Depreciation	−100,000	($50,000 recapturable)
Adjusted basis	$ 50,000	

When Margaret sold her apartment building, the selling price was $200,000. Her gain was, therefore, $150,000.

Selling price	$200,000
Basis	− 50,000
Gain	$150,000

Since she had held the property for more than a year and otherwise qualified, most of that gain came under the capital gains rule. However, because of recapture, $50,000 was considered ordinary income.

Total gain	$150,000
Recaptured depreciation (ordinary income)	− 50,000
Capital gain	$100,000

Margaret sold on the installment method. She received a $30,000 payment in the year of sale with additional payments over the next 5 years until her full contract price was reached. How is the gain reported for each installment—as capital gains or as recaptured income?

The $50,000 of ordinary income must all be reported *first*. This means that the taxable portion of the $30,000 initial payment is taxed as ordinary income, as is the taxable portion of the next payment, until the $50,000 ordinary income from recapture of depreciation has been accounted for. After that, the taxable portion of each payment receives capital gains treatment.

This reporting of ordinary income first can work a hardship for some investors who have large amounts of recaptured depreciation, and use of the installment method for them should be carefully considered.

Since only two payments are required to qualify for the installment method, it is possible to spread the two payments out over an extremely short period of time.

A taxpayer who is closing a sale near the end of the year may have many of the benefits of both the installment method and a cash sale. The rule states that the payments must be spread over at least two years, but it does not say how far apart they must be. A year-end sale can qualify if, for example, the sale is on December 31st, even if the second and *last* installment is on January 2d of the next year.

If Sarah were selling her property in a cash sale at the end of December and were receiving a gain of $50,000 in the year of sale, she might reduce that gain down to $25,000 in the year of sale and $25,000 in the next year by using the installment method. She could do this even though the first payment of $25,000 and the second payment of $25,000 were received only days apart, by having each fall in a different year. The tax saving here, because of spreading the income over two years, could be substantial.

The installment method is available to all sellers of real estate.

It does not matter whether the seller is an occasional investor or a dealer in real estate (see Chapter 7 for a definition of a dealer). The installment method is available to both.

DEFERRED-PAYMENT SALES

The deferred-payment method of reporting gain on the sale of property can be a real benefit for those who receive more than 30 percent in payments in the first year and do not qualify for the installment plan sale. It may not be, however, as advantageous as the installment plan. (We'll go into some of the differences in a moment.)

Here is how the deferred-payment plan works:

If the total payments in the year of the sale exceed 30 percent, then the taxpayer may not report the sale on the installment plan. Normally, this means that the taxpayer must pay the tax on the full recognized gain in the year that it is received. An exception to this rule exists when there is an obligation received as part of the gain and there is a difference between the fair market value of the obligation and its face value.

For example, it is often the case that a seller will take back a second mortgage on a transaction. The face value of the mortgage may state that it is worth, say, $10,000. But the condition of the second-mortgage market at that time may be such that if the seller tries to immediately dispose of the mortgage, its fair market value might be only 60 percent of its face value.

When the fair market value of an obligation taken as payment is less than the face value, the difference does not have to be reported as gain before it is actually collected.

In our example, this means that if the fair market value of the mortgage taken back by the seller as part of the selling price is $6,000, even though the face value is $10,000, only this $6,000 need be reported immediately as gain. The remainder need only be reported as it is received.

The advantage here should be fairly obvious. By spreading the taxable gain out over a period of years, it may be possible to pay a lower percentage of tax on it in each year. In this sense the deferred-payment sale's benefits are similar to those for the installment plan.

There are, however, some disadvantages. One has to do with capital gains.

In deferred-payment sales, if the taxpayer is an individual, that portion of the gain received in later years may not be treated as capital gains, but instead must be treated as ordinary income.

Losing some capital gains treatment is a big disadvantage of the deferred-payment sale. To understand how this works it is necessary to draw a distinction between gain received in the year and gain received in later years.

All obligations worth face value received in the year of sale are treated as cash.

The difference between the face value and the fair market value must be reported as ordinary income when received in later years.

If a seller receives a mortgage for $10,000 with a fair market value of $6,000, the $6,000 is treated as cash received. If the taxpayer qualifies for capital gains treatment on the property, the $6,000 may be taken as a capital gain (or loss). The $4,000 difference between the cash value and the fair market value on the mortgage, however, when it is received in later years, *must* be treated as ordinary income. (See next page.) This can pose a certain dilemma for the taxpayer.

If our taxpayer were to sell the property and receive a mortgage back for $10,000 and if the sale qualified as a capital gain, by valuing the note at face value at the time of sale, our taxpayer could pay capital gains on the full $10,000. On the other hand, if our taxpayer declares that the note has a fair market value of only $6,000, then he or she can take capital gains on only this amount. The remaining $4,000 may not be treated as capital gains. It will be ordinary income when it is received. Which is the best course of action to take?

This is a matter for each taxpayer to decide with the aid of an attorney or an accountant. It should be noted, however, that this problem does not exist if the taxpayer has not held the property for at least a year or otherwise does not qualify for capital gains, since it would then be or-dinary income in either case.

When payments on the obligation are collected in later years, part of the payment is considered taxable while the remainder is considered a return of capital.

Consider this problem. If our taxpayer declared that $6,000 was the face value of a $10,000 mortgage, he or she would pay tax on this $6,000 in the year of sale. As we have said, the tax on the remaining $4,000 would be paid as ordinary income as it was received. Now, let us suppose that the mortgage was to be paid over 10 years in payments of $1,000 each year (exclusive of interest). When our taxpayer received the first payment of $1,000, did tax have to be paid on the full sum or only a part of it?

The answer is, only a part of it. The taxpayer paid the tax on a portion of the full mortgage in the year of sale. Now, only that portion of each payment that represents that part of the mortgage on which no tax was paid is subject to tax in the year it is received.

The ratio of the fair market value at the time of sale to the face value of the obligation is the same ratio applied to each payment to determine which portion is exempt from tax as a return of capital and which portion is taxable income.

This may sound complex, but is really quite simple. Sally, the taxpayer in our example, valued the mortgage at 60 percent of face and paid tax on this amount, which means that 40 percent was not taxed. Thus 40 percent of each payment ($400) is taxable as ordinary income in the year received.

Exhibit 15-2 and Table 15-1 show how the entire transaction looked.

EXHIBIT 15-2

Cash		$10,000
First mortgage assumed by buyer, therefore valued at face		30,000
Second mortgage taken by seller	$10,000	
Discount—40%	−4,000	
		+ 6,000
Fair market value of mortgage		
		$46,000
		−20,000
Sally's adjusted basis in the property		$26,000

As should be apparent, the proportioning of payment between return of capital and income is fairly straightforward, as is almost the entire deferred-payment method. The only area that may be tricky has to do with the valuation of the obligation.

TABLE 15-1 Accounting for the Difference between the Face Value and the Fair Market Value of the Mortgage Sally Received (the Discount)*

Year after sale	Payment received	Less 60% already reported	40% to be reported as ordinary income
1	$1,000	$600	$400
2	$1,000	$600	$400
3	$1,000	$600	$400
4	$1,000	$600	$400
5	$1,000	$600	$400
6	$1,000	$600	$400
7	$1,000	$600	$400
8	$1,000	$600	$400
9	$1,000	$600	$400
10	$1,000	$600	$400

* $600 of each $1,000 is exempt as a return on investment. $400 of each payment is considered ordinary income and is subject to tax.

It is up to the taxpayer to state the fair market value of the obligation. Only in very unusual circumstances will an obligation be considered to have no fair market value at all.

Since the determination of the fair market value is up to the taxpayer, in order to put off tax until later years there may be a tendency to place the fair market value very low or to declare that the obligation has no fair market value.

This can work against the taxpayer. In no cases that we have dealt with has the IRS allowed the taxpayer to declare no fair market value for a mortgage at the time of sale. In general, the taxpayer must justify a declaration of fair market value. In our last example with Sally, she would have to show that the second-mortgage market at the time of sale would indeed require a 40 percent discount on an immediate sale.

16

Tax Shelters and the Vacation Home

If the taxpayer can show that he or she comes within
the hobby rule guidelines, then a rebuttal may be
made to an IRS assertion that a particular piece of
property is for pleasure and not for business use.   page 186

If anyone uses the vacation home and does not pay
fair rental value or uses the home under a reciprocal
arrangement whether or not a fair rental is charged,
it is presumed to be personal use.   page 187

In the past, many agents sold vacation homes to investors as both items of personal pleasure and tax shelters. The investor would purchase such property assuming that he or she could use the home part of the year for recreation and vacation purposes and rent it out for the other part of the year — claiming the entire property as an investment and taking normal investment deductions. This meant that many investors anticipated deducting not only property taxes and mortgage interest, but also maintenance, utilities, and depreciation. When these expenses were added in to a property that was rented for only part of the year, the expenses very often exceeded the income. Thus a loss resulted, and the investor deducted this from his or her ordinary income—a tax shelter.

We have heard of agents who told their investor clients that as long as they used the vacation home for personal purposes less than 50 percent of the time, they could write off the entire property. Others may have suggested that as long as the house was rented out for just a few weeks a year, it became an investment and deductions for depreciation, utilities, maintenance, and other normal investment-deductible items were allowed. Unfortunately, nothing could be farther from the truth.

In most cases a vacation home may not be considered an investment for tax purposes.

While property taxes and mortgage interest may still be deducted for a vacation home (as they are for any real estate), the other items, such as depreciation, maintenance, utilities, and so on, usually may not. Let us consider when they can be deducted.

Although the rules for vacation homes have not in reality changed much over the years, the Tax Reform Act of 1976 spelled them out very specifically. This has resulted in a stricter interpretation of the law by the IRS than we have seen in the past.

The reform act divided up the use of vacation homes into three areas: rental use of 14 days or less; great personal use; and personal use of 14 days or less (or 10 percent of the time rented, whichever is greater). We'll discuss each of these separately, but first let us consider what a vacation home really is.

In its broadest sense, a vacation home may be a house, condominium, boat, apartment, or other similar property that is used for both personal and rental use.

It is important here to understand that a vacation home need not be a house or cottage. A houseboat may qualify just as easily.

RENTAL USE OF 14 DAYS OR LESS A YEAR

If an investor owns a vacation home and rents it out for 14 days or less a year, the taxpayer may take no deductions of an investment nature on the property (other than the normal property taxes and mortgage interest, which are always deductible) and the taxpayer need not declare the income received on his or her income tax form under gross income.

For those who intend purchasing a vacation home strictly for personal use, this is a real bonus. By simply renting out the property two weeks a year, tax-free income can be generated.

GREAT PERSONAL USE

If the taxpayer uses the vacation home for more than 14 days a year or 10 percent of the time rented, whichever is greater, special limitations take effect. These limitations do not allow the deduction of expenses over and above rental income. They do not allow for a tax shelter.

Susan purchases a vacation home (see Exhibit 16-1). She rents out the home for 5 months of the year and uses it herself for 2 months. The gross rental income from the home is $4,000. In addition, Susan has the following expenses: property taxes, $1,200; mortgage interest, $1,400. There are also other expenses attributable only to the rental period: utilities, $400; maintenance, $600; advertising, $100; depreciation, $1,000.

EXHIBIT 16-1

Susan's Vacation Home:

Gross income for year		$4,000
Expenses:		
Property taxes	$1,200	
Mortgage interest	1,400	
Utilities	400	
Maintenance	600	
Advertising	100	
Depreciation	1,000	
	$4,700	

If this were an investment other than a vacation home, we would simply deduct expenses from income, giving us a loss of $700. This loss would be deductible from Susan's ordinary income, giving her a tax shelter.

However, because it is a vacation home under the rules we are considering, Susan may not do this. Instead, the following computations are made:

First, mortgage interest and property taxes are added:

Mortgage interest	$1,400
Property taxes	+1,200
	$2,600

This figure is now subtracted from the gross income:

Gross income	$4,000
Less	−2,600
Expense limit	$1,400

Excess Expense Limit

The maximum amount of rental expenses that Susan can deduct on the property is $1,400, and they must be deducted in this order: maintenance, utilities, and all other expenses other than depreciation first, then depreciation.

Maintenance	$ 600
Utilities	400
Advertising	100
	$1,100

This is now subtracted from the limit on rental expenses:

Expense limit	$1,400
Expenses other than depreciation	− 1,100
Allowable depreciation	$ 300

The $300 remaining is the total amount of depreciation that Susan can deduct on the property, regardless of the fact that her normal depreciation would be $1,000.

The result, as should be evident, is that while expenses can be used to offset gross income so that there is no taxable income, expenses cannot be used to offset gross income to show a loss. And without a loss, there is no tax shelter.

A final word of explanation here should be given in regard to the method for calculating rental expenses such as maintenance and utilities when the vacation home is used partly for rental purposes and partly for personal use. The rental expenses are limited to that portion of the total expenses that bears the same ratio to such expenses as the number of days per year the vacation home is actually rented out bears to the total number of days per year the home is actually used for all purposes. This is a complicated but necessary way of saying something very simple. An illustration should clarify it.

If a vacation home is used for all purposes for 100 days out of the year and rented out only 70 days, then the ratio of days rented to days used is 7 to 10, or 70 percent of the time. Deductible rental expenses, then, are simply in a ratio of 7 to 10 (or 70%) to total expenses. If utilities are $1,000, then $700 can be deducted as rental expense. (The remaining $300 is attributable to personal use and is not deductible.)

PERSONAL USE LIMITED TO 14 DAYS A YEAR OR 10 PERCENT OF THE RENTAL

Thus far, we've discussed the situation where (1) the investor uses the property almost entirely for personal use, and (2) where the investor uses the property a large portion of the time for personal use. Now, let us consider a different situation.

When personal use is limited to a maximum of 14 days a year or 10 percent of the rental time, whichever is less, the IRS hobby rules apply.

The hobby rules were originally set up to protect the government from subsidizing a taxpayer's hobby. For example, a taxpayer might be keenly interested in model railroading and open up a tiny shop where he or she buys and sells model trains. However, because it is a hobby, the taxpayer does not operate the business to make a profit, but rather for pleasure. In such a case the business could lose money year after year; such losses very frequently used to be deducted from regular income. To prevent this abuse, the hobby rules were born. They seek to determine whether the individual was actually in business or was merely enjoying a hobby.

Losses from a hobby are not deductible. Losses from a business are. To claim a loss on a vacation home, the taxpayer must prove it is operated as a business.

The hobby rules are fairly complicated, and it is not necessary for us to go into great detail on them here. They include several tests which can be applied to a piece of property to determine whether it is for business or pleasure use. One test is whether the property has shown a profit in two out of five consecutive years (subject to certain conditions). Most real estate would fail this test since, after depreciation is figured in, most real estate shows a paper loss year after year.

The law, however, does allow the taxpayer another test, and that is in the form of certain guidelines to be applied to the taxpayer. These include, among others, the guideline that if the taxpayer expects that the asset's value will increase, it might be considered a business or investment. Other guidelines center around the taxpayer's expertise, his track record of success in other similar activities, his financial status, and so on.

If the taxpayer can show that he or she comes within the hobby rule guidelines, then a rebuttal may be made to an IRS assertion that a particular piece of property is for pleasure and not for business use.

The preparation of a rebuttal to the IRS on the hobby rule guidelines is a fit subject for an attorney, and if the situation arises, an agent should certainly advise an investor-client to consult with one. What is important here is to understand that even if the use of a vacation home is on a very limited basis, there is a good chance that the IRS will presume it is a hobby and *not allow* those deductions that make it into a tax shelter.

Finally, there is the case where the taxpayer never uses the property for personal use but only for business use. If the property is a condominium or a house in a city, there is little chance the IRS could argue that it is not an investment. But if it is a condominium at the seashore or the mountains or any other resort area, there might be some difficulty.

It could be argued that the taxpayer *intended* pleasure use or intends to use it for pleasure in the future.

Even in cases of no personal use, the *hobby rules still would be used.* It seems likely, however, that a taxpayer could justify his or her assertion that a piece of property was owned as an investment and not for pleasure if he or she *never* made personal use of it.

A word of caution about what constitutes personal and rental use: Rental use is when the property is rented out for *full fair rental value.* This means that a charge is made and payment received.

If anyone uses the vacation home and does not pay fair rental value or uses the home under a reciprocal arrangement whether or not a fair rental is charged, it is presumed to be personal use.

It doesn't matter if someone uses a vacation home for just a day or even an hour. Using the home at all without paying fair rental value is considered personal use.

It should be clear from this discussion that an agent advising a client to buy a vacation home because it can be used as a tax shelter is on very shaky ground. If the agent wants to give such advice, he or she had best consult a tax attorney on the specific piece of property to see what likelihood there is that the IRS will consider the property to be for personal or pleasure use rather than investment use.

17

Tax Considerations in Handling Options, Leases, Wraparounds, and Contracts of Sale

OPTIONS

An option, as agents and investors are aware, is a device whereby a purchaser can "tie up" a piece of property for a period of time without actually purchasing it. The option gives its holder, who is called an "optionee," the exclusive right to purchase a piece of property for a limited period of time at a specified price. Unlike a contract of sale, an option is strictly a one-way agreement. The optionee has the right to purchase or not purchase within the time limits at the specified price. The seller, who is called the "optionor," must sell if the optionee elects to exercise the option. It is helpful to think of the option in contrast to a contract of sale, which actually binds *both* parties.

The option has several tax considerations, but the one most common has to do with the seller or optionor.

By giving an option to purchase his or her property instead of actually selling it, an optionor can receive a payment, have free use of the money, and yet not report it as income until a later tax year.

Suppose Rita decides to give Bob an option on her apartment building instead of selling it to him. The option is for $5,000, and the purchase price is $200,000. Rita reports her income on a calendar-year basis and gives the option to Bob in June 1978 for one year.

If Bob does not exercise his option until June of the next year, 1979, Rita does not have to report the $5,000 of income in 1978, the year in which she receives it. If Bob decides not to exercise his option at all but instead to forfeit the $5,000, this also need not be reported until the full term of the option has expired. The only way Rita would need to report the money, in our example, in the year in which it was received would be if Bob exercised his option early, say in December 1978. Then it would count toward that year's taxable income.

The advantage to a seller who has high income in a particular year but anticipates lower income in the next is obvious. But there is yet another tax advantage of the option, although the circumstances where it may be used are limited. This is called the "successive option."

The Successive Option

Let us say that an investor owns a large number of lots and wishes to sell them all to a developer. If the investor wishes to defer taxes on the sale over a period of years, he or she can receive only 30 percent or less of the sale price in the first year and must receive the remainder in one or more payments. This 30 percent installment method limitation can be avoided by using successive options. The investor, instead of selling the lots to the developer outright, gives the developer a series of options, one on each lot (assuming they are contiguous), a condition of the options being that each one can be exercised only if and when the previous one has been exercised. These are successive options.

The exercise of each option becomes a separate transaction. This means that more than 30 percent of the total property can be sold in a year without the sale prices of the total properties being taxed in that year. For example, 50 percent of the options can be exercised in the initial year. Only the gain on those 50 percent need to reported. Gain on the remaining 50 percent need be reported only as the options on those lots are also exercised.

The use of successive options, in addition to tax advantages, carries with it risks. These include the possibility that the buyer-optionee might not exercise the option on later lots. Thus, the property might end up not all being sold — a situation that would not occur if the property had been sold as a single unit at the outset. Another problem is that the taxpayer might be considered a dealer. Anyone contemplating the use of a successive option should check with an attorney familiar with the procedure to learn fully what the risks are.

While these are the primary tax advantages of the option, the agent and investor should be aware of the tax rules that apply.

Tax Consequences When an Option Is Exercised

For the optionee or buyer, the holding period for capital gains treatment on the property (for its eventual resale) begins *the day following the exercise of the option* if the title passes upon exercise.

It is important to understand that the holding period does not begin when the option is first given.

For the seller or optionor, gain or loss from the sale occurs when the sale actually takes place (normally when title changes hands). It does not occur simply when the option is exercised (although normally the two occur simultaneously).

For the seller or optionor the holding period for capital gains (currently one year) is not affected by the option. The holding period begins when the seller purchases the property and ends when he or she sells it, regardless of any options given.

Normally, the option provides that the option money will be part of the purchase price, but not always. It can be the case that all or a portion of the option money is *in addition* to the purchase price. This has important tax considerations for the seller-optionor.

All of that portion of the option money which is *in addition* to the sale price is considered ordinary income and is taxed in the year received.

Large Option Payments May Defeat Tax Advantages

In some cases the amount of money paid for the option can be very large in relation to the total price of the property. If the option money seems overly large to the IRS in relation to the total price paid, the government may decide that it was not really an option but a sale with an agreement to pay the remainder of the purchase price at a later date. In this case the tax advantages of the option would probably be lost.

If the Option Is Not Exercised

For the optionee, or buyer, the nonexercise of an option can have significant tax considerations. The option is treated as an asset and has the same character as the property it relates to.

Unless the optionee is a dealer in real estate (or a dealer in options), the option on investment property is considered a capital asset. This means that if the option runs for over a year it is subject to capital gains treatment. The result is:

An option *for more than a year* that is not exercised can only be reported as a *long-term loss* by the optionee. (If the property on which the option given is a personal residence, no loss is deductible.)

Since most optionees would prefer to have short-term losses (which can be applied to offset short-term gains—those treated as ordinary income), it is usually to their advantage to sell the option at a nominal fee before a year is up. In this manner the option is treated as a short-term or ordinary loss.

Occasionally the owner of an option (the optionee) will not purchase and not exercise the option but will instead sell it to a third party. This is frequently the case when the value of the property has appreciated significantly. Rather than go through the bother and expense of a purchase of the property and subsequent sale, the optionee simply sells the option for the increase in value to the property.

The gain thus realized (or the loss, as we just saw) is treated according to the manner in which the property would be treated if it were purchased. Assuming no dealer is involved and it is a capital asset, if the option is held for under one year, the gain on sale is considered a short-term capital gain and treated as ordinary income. If the option is held for over a year, the gain is subject to capital gains treatment.

Care must be taken in selling or transferring an option that the method used is clear-cut and precise. The danger is that the IRS might interpret the sale of the option as, in reality, the purchase and subsequent sale of the property.

If the IRS interprets the sale of an option as a purchase and resale of the property, there can be no capital gains treatment, since the holding period for the property begins the day after the purchase (not when the option is given) and, presumably, the purchase and sale on such an agreement occur simultaneously.

Occasionally it may happen that the optionor (seller) wants the option back from the optionee. In order to get it back the optionor may not only have to return the option money, but also have to pay a penalty. This penalty would probably be considered ordinary income to the optionee regardless of how long he or she has held the property.

For the optionor or seller, the nonexercise of the option is treated very simply as ordinary income. If the payment is to be part of the purchase price, it is reported in the year in which the time for exercising the option expires.

THE "WRAPAROUND" OR ALL-INCLUSIVE DEED OF TRUST (AITD)

A wraparound is a financing device that makes use of an existing low interest rate mortgage. Rather than pay off the existing mortgage, the owner takes a new mortgage (second) on the property and makes payments to the lender of this second, who in turn makes the payments on the existing mortgage. This ability of the lender of the second to control the payment of the first is the additional security which allows that second lender to make a much higher and more substantial loan than otherwise would be available.

In the past the wraparound in the sale of a piece of property was frequently used to allow the purchaser to make a large prepayment of interest, usually when the second lender was also the seller. This tax advantage, however, was lost when the 1976 Tax Reform Act provided that no prepaid interest at all was deductible. (See Chapter 4 for a further discussion.)

Recently, "wraps" have again come into favor, though not for tax reasons. Now, they may allow a seller to sell property without disturbing an existing low-interest loan.

LEASES

While at first glance it may appear that there are no tax considerations with regard to leases, since title to property does not change hands, upon closer examination this does not prove to be the case. There are in fact many tax considerations, of which we will consider six.

Basically, for the lessee (tenant) and lessor (landlord), the tax rules are that the lessee deducts the rent as an expense

as it is paid. **The lessor counts the rental money as income as soon as it is received.**

The tax rules produce some strikingly different consequences for lessee and lessor, as we shall soon see.

Advance Rental Payments

Advance payments of rent are treated as income when received.

In many leases it is common for the lessee to pay the lessor a certain sum of money, frequently the last month's rent, in advance. The lessor in such a case must treat the money as income *when it is received,* even if it does not apply to rent for many months or years in the future.

The lessee may not treat the advance payment of rent as a deduction until it actually becomes applied toward rent.

If a commercial tenant leases a store at $1,000 a month for 24 months and pays the first and last months' rent in advance, the following results occur: The lessor immediately treats the $2,000 received as income. The lessee treats $1,000 of the amount paid as a deduction, since it is applied to the first month's rent immediately. The lessee, however, has to wait until the twenty-fourth month to count the other $1,000 as a deduction, since it may not be applied toward rent until then.

Security Deposits

Security deposits are usually money paid to a lessor by a lessee to insure that the lessee will live up to his or her obligations under a lease. The most common item they usually cover is damage to the premises. They normally also contain a provision that in the event the lessee lives up to his or her obligations, the money will be returned and if not, it will be forfeited.

If a lessor receives a security deposit and places it in a special account to which he or she does not have personal access, normally it need not be reported as income until the lease expires and the money is forfeited (if, in fact, it is).

For the lessee, the security deposit is similarly handled. The lessee may not deduct the security deposit (if it is given under conditions similar to those just described) when it is paid or at any time during the lease. The lessee may deduct the deposit only when the lease is terminated and the deposit forfeited (if it is).

Bonuses

In some cases a lessee must pay a bonus to a lessor in order to obtain a lease. This may be the case when the property is in a particularly desirable location. The bonus is handled in entirely different ways for lessee and lessor.

For the lessee, the bonus deduction must be fully amortized over the term of the lease. If a lessee rents a store for $12,000 a year for 5 years and in addition pays a $5,000 bonus to obtain the lease, the lessee must amortize the bonus and deduct it over the 5-year term of the lease. This means a $1,000 deduction each year.

For the lessor, bonuses are simply treated as rental income and declared in the year in which they are received.

Cancellation Bonuses

There is another kind of bonus, and that one is paid when a lease is canceled. Either party may pay the other a bonus for the privilege of having the lease canceled.

When the lessee pays the lessor a cancellation bonus, the tax considerations are simple. The lessor declares the bonus to be income in the year received and the lessee declares it an immediate expense (since this lease is immediately canceled).

On the other hand, when a lessor pays a lessee a bonus to quit, the tax handling is a bit more complicated. For the lessor, a cancellation bonus paid to a lessee may not be deducted immediately.

A cancellation bonus paid by a lessor to a lessee must be capitalized and deducted over a period determined by the reason for the lease cancellation. For example, if the lessor has canceled the lease in order to release the property to a new tenant, the cancellation bonus must be fully amortized over the full term of the *new* lease. On the other hand, if the lessor has canceled the lease with no intention of re-leasing (perhaps he or she intends to occupy the property), it must be fully amortized over what would have been the remaining period of the *old* lease had it not been canceled. And finally, if the lessor has canceled the lease in order to build on the property for his or her own use, the bonus must be amortized and deducted over the life of the new building. (In the event a lessor cancels a lease and then sells, the bonus given is added to the property's basis before gain or loss is calculated.)

It is not quite so complicated from the viewpoint of the lessee. If the lessee receives a bonus on a lease for a cancellation, the bonus is treated as a capital gain if the lease is for over a year. For under a year it is treated as short-term capital gain which is ordinary income.

If the tenant is a "dealer" in leases or one who makes leases and holds them for sale to others, the bonus is always treated as ordinary income.

Lease Expenses

Frequently there will be expenses for both parties in obtaining a lease. The lessor may have agent's fees to pay, and the lessee may have attorney's fees, to name only two items. These expenses are handled in the same way for lessee and lessor. Both lessee and lessor must normally capitalize expenses and fully amortize them over the entire period of the lease.

Net Leases

Many commercial leases today are "net" leases, of one type or another, that require the tenant to pay the lessor's property taxes, insurance, and other items in addition to normal rent.

For the lessor additional payments must be treated as rental income. For the lessee, additional payments are treated simply as additional rent expense and are deductible in the same manner as normal rent.

It should be noted that although the additional payments are treated as income for the lessor, he or she is normally still entitled to a deduction for the item on which they are paid. For example, the lessee may pay the lessor's taxes directly or indirectly. The lessor must then count this money as additional rent payment but normally may still take a deduction for the taxes.

Ground Leases

The type of lease we have been discussing thus far might be termed a "simple" lease. The owner of a piece of propety simply leases or gives the right of its use to a tenant. There is another type of lease, however, which is occasionally used in commercial and industrial properties as an alternative to an outright sale—the ground lease.

The ground lease is simply one in which the tenant leases the land only and not the building. Most frequently it is used where the lessee (tenant) intends to construct a new building on the land, such as a restaurant or gas station. In these circumstances the building belongs to the lessee, the land to the lessor. This kind of lease may also be made with an existing building where the owner of the property sells the existing building to an investor and then leases the land it is upon.

There are several advantages to this type of arrangement. For the lessee, there is usually less money required to complete the transaction, since only the building is being purchased and not the land. This frequently means that greater leverage in financing is obtainable. Second, there is an important tax consideration.

In a ground lease, the lessee can depreciate almost the entire investment.

The building, which the lessee owns, is depreciable. In addition, the money paid in rent for use of the land is deductible, and the result is that the lessee is, in effect, depreciating the land as well. Of course, the lessee does not normally own the land at the end of the lease, so that the payments are actually for only the use of the land during the term.

For the lessor there are also advantages. There is a steady income stream from the property, something that otherwise would not normally exist from bare land. In addition, if a building already exists, there is an immediate cash payment. Also, the lessor may obtain additional funds through a leasehold mortgage or by borrowing on or selling the rights to the property once the lease expires.

The disadvantages to the lessor include the fact that he or she will not be able to take a depreciation deduction on the property (since the lessee owns the depreciable part—the building), which means that income from the lease will not be sheltered but will be taxed as ordinary income.

THE CONTRACT OF SALE

The contract of sale, or "land contract of sale," as it is also known, is a financing device with a new twist. Until recently it was occasionally used primarily to help buyers of land who did not have enough cash to make an appropriate down payment.

Under the contract of sale, a seller retains title by deed to the property and also retains liability under existing mortgages. The buyer agrees by means of a contract to pay the seller usually enough money to cover all existing mortgages, plus an additional amount to be applied toward a down payment. When enough money has been paid to the seller to equal an agreed-upon down payment, the buyer refinances (either getting a new loan or assuming the existing loan) and the seller transfers the deed to the property.

In the last few years, however, the contract of sale has been increasingly used to allow buyers to retain the benefit of older existing low interest rate financing. This has come about because of an interesting court ruling in California in 1976.

In the past contracts of sale were infrequently used because most real estate mortgages contained an "alienation" or "due on sale" clause. This was a clause that provided that the payment of the mortgage would be accelerated in the event the borrower alienated or sold the property. It in effect meant that the lender had the option of demanding full payment of the mortgage upon sale of the property. Lenders have increasingly insisted on such a clause to protect themselves from the possibility that the property will be turned over to a party who is a bad credit risk. (It has also been suggested by many that another motive was to collect additional financing charges by transferring the loan from one party to another.)

An owner who had a mortgage containing such a clause could not sell his or her property under a contract of sale, because this would constitute an alienation and make the mortgage immediately due and payable. In 1976, however, in Lassen County, California, the courts held that such an alienation clause in a trust deed was not always enforceable under a contract of sale. The court concerned itself with the question of whether or not the seller retained a substantial equity in the property.

For example, let us suppose a seller sells a piece of property for $100,000 under a contract of sale. The seller has an existing first mortgage of $50,000 on which there is an alienation clause. The buyer puts down $20,000 in cash and the remaining $30,000 under the contract over a period of years. Since the seller's equity (30,000) is so substantial, the presumption undoubtedly is that he or she will keep a watchful eye on the property and the lender has no real justification for enforcing the alienation clause.

On the other hand, if the existing mortgage is $79,000 and the buyer puts down $20,000, leaving the owner with an equity of merely $1,000, the presumption probably is that there is not sufficient equity to insure that the seller will take proper care of the property, and the alienation clause might be enforced, regardless of the fact that there is a contract of sale. (There have been more recent decisions affecting this outcome.)

The 1976 ruling has led to the greatly expanded use of the contract of sale in California and, as other states adopt similar rulings, in other parts of the country. The benefits of such "financing with a new twist" can best be seen by an example:

If a seller has a piece of property worth $75,000, with an existing low interest rate $40,000 mortgage, previously the only way a sale could be made was to have the buyer get a new mortgage, in which case the lender invariably raised the interest rate to the current high. Now, under a contract of sale in California, the seller can sell the property over a long-term installment period—say 15 or 20 years. The buyer can give the seller a substantial down payment, say $20,000, then pay the balance owed ($15,000) over the long term. The net effect is a lower mortgage rate for the buyer.

Price	$75,000
Existing mortgage	$40,000 at 5% interest
Cash down	20,000
Amount paid in installments over 20 years	15,000 at 9% interest
	$75,000

For the seller the advantage is a sale in a time of tight money and high interest rates. Of course, should interest rates drop, such sales would lose their attractiveness. (It should be noted that to protect the buyer and seller, the agreements under such a contract should be handled by a competent attorney.)

For tax purposes, the property is sold upon executing the contract of sale (at the time the buyer acquires interest in it), not at the time the deed is finally transferred by the seller. This means that the buyer who has the contract has legal title and is entitled to all the normal real estate deductions that go with the sale. Since the seller, however, also has an interest in the property (equitable title), the seller may take these deductions if he or she actually pays them. Buyer and seller may not, however, both deduct the same taxes, interest, and expenses.

18

Modern Real Estate Syndication

The old expression, "a day late or a dollar short," has never been applied more aptly than it has been to real estate. With prices in all areas of the country rising rapidly, investors are constantly faced with the frustration of seeing good deals pass them by because they don't have enough cash to act. And if they wait the years to get the cash, the deal will have long since faded. Agents, too, are a party to this frustration as they see potential investment deals dissolve because their investors are too "small" for the property.

One solution to this frustrating problem is through syndication, or the formation of a limited partnership. This is a vehicle which small investors can use to buy large properties. It is a particularly helpful tool for agents, also. By organizing syndicates, they can generate new clients and deals. And in addition to these benefits, the syndicate also offers distinct tax advantages to participants. The formation of a syndicate, or limited partnership, however, is a complicated legal procedure. It must conform to all applicable state and federal laws, a description of which would fill many volumes. Consequently, forming a syndicate or limited partnership should not be undertaken without the aid of an attorney familiar with the laws of the state in which it is being formed as well as with federal law on the subject. This chapter, however, will give the agent and the investor an insight into some of the tax advantages (and problems) that can be associated with syndication.

THE LIMITED PARTNERSHIP

A syndicate in real estate is, generally, a "limited partnership." In order to understand what this term means, it is first necessary to understand what an unlimited or "general partnership" is.

A partnership, most simply, is two or more individuals joined together for a legitimate purpose. The partnership agreement is governed by the laws of the state in which the partnership is registered. In most states, a *general* partnership has unlimited liability. "Unlimited liability" means that in the event of a business loss or any other loss, including personal injury, involving the partnership, each partner is liable for that loss. A general partnership is most frequently used when each partner actively participates in the business and is able to know from moment to moment what position the business is in and how his or her interest is faring— that is, is able to protect himself or herself (see Figure 18-1).

A limited partnership normally offers limited liability.

A limited partnership is much like a corporation. The limited partner frequently is limited in his or her liability to the total amount required

FIG. 18-1 General partnership.

to be invested. In most states, if the partnership agreement binding the participants together specifically states that the limited partners are not liable for more than their original investment, then those limited partners are not liable for the partnership's business losses, even if the losses are due to a personal injury suit (see Figure 18-2).

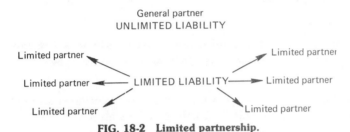

FIG. 18-2 Limited partnership.

The idea of a limited partnership comes out of the fact that there are people who simply want to invest their money but don't want to be involved in the day-to-day operation of a business. They aren't on hand to be constantly vigilant over the actions of the partnership, and consequently they need to have their liability limited.

Every limited partnership must have at least one general partner who assumes unlimited liability.

If limited partners were the only participants in the partnership, then there would be no liability whatsoever; there would be no one in a position of accountability. Consequently, every partnership must have at least one general partner who is liable for all the losses of the partnership.

The syndicate must be a viable entity.

A further word of caution regarding the creation of syndicates. In some cases individuals have sought to *totally* limit the liability yet retain the tax advantages (which we'll discuss in just a moment) of the syndicate.

The usual method of accomplishing this is to have the general partner be a corporation instead of an individual. Since corporations have limited liability, and since the other participants would be limited partners, the overall liability would be limited.

The problem here is that unless the corporation which becomes the general partner is a viable entity (an actual functioning corporation, not just a paper organization), and unless that corporation actually has a real interest in the syndicate's business, the IRS is likely to treat the entire partnership as if it were a corporation. This means it will be taxed as a corporation, not as a partnership, and the tax advantages (which we'll discuss shortly) will be lost. To avoid this possibility, it is probably better if an *individual* is the general partner; in many states, any adult may be a general partner. The IRS wants to see somebody "sticking his neck out." If the syndicate is properly organized, it is usually worth the risk.

The number of partners who may participate in a limited partnership is determined by state and, in some cases, federal law.

In most states partnerships with more than a certain number of individuals must register and conform to strict state regulation. Each state determines the size and regulation of these partnerships.

The individual who organizes the limited partnership is usually the general partner. He or she normally finds the property that will be purchased, in a real estate syndication, and then finds the limited partners who will put up the money for the purchase.

In many states, an individual does not need to be licensed to participate in a syndication.

For agents, syndication offers the opportunity of calling together several clients, both licensed agents and nonprofessionals, who are limited in their investment cash but together can afford a large piece of property. The agent frequently can both be the general partner and also collect a commission, and so syndicates can be a source of new income. (Note: The above is only the case for intrastate private offerings where no federal or state regulations prohibit it.)

TAX ADVANTAGES OF SYNDICATES

No "Dealer" Problem for Capital Gains

An investor who wants to get deeply involved in real estate is often stopped by the fact that if an investor buys and sells more than five properties a year, the IRS frequently will classify that investor as a dealer. A dealer is not entitled to capital gains treatment on sales or to tax-free exchanges—an enormous disadvantage when selling and buying property.

On the other hand, an investor can join as many partnerships as desired, as long as participation is as a *limited partner,* and have little fear of being labeled a dealer. When you consider that any given limited partnership may buy and sell a half dozen properties in a year, an investor joining five such syndicates could participate in a great number of sales and purchases without dealer problems. (A word of caution: A *general partner* who participates in five or more sales and purchases in a year probably will be considered a dealer.)

Pass-through benefits allow partners to take full advantage of paper losses and positive cash flows.

In a corporation, if there is a loss, it goes on the corporate tax return and does not directly benefit the stockholders. Similarly, in a corporation, a profit goes to the corporate tax return and then is paid to the stock-holders in dividends, which are normally taxable. In a limited partner-ship, both losses and profits pass through directly to the limited partners. Let's take an example. Suppose we have a syndicate with five partners. They purchase a piece of investment property which has $10,000 of income, $5,000 total expenses, and $10,000 of depreciation.

Income		$10,000
Less:		
Total expenses	$ 5,000	
Depreciation	10,000	− 15,000
Paper loss		($ 5,000)

The investment shows a loss on paper (largely because of the depreciation) of $5,000. The five partners now may allocate this loss among themselves, getting 20 percent each, for example. That means that each partner gets a $1,000 loss to use as a deduction against ordinary income. For a partner in a 50 percent tax bracket this means a cash saving of $500, or in the 25 percent bracket, $250, of money that would otherwise have to be paid in taxes.

In addition, the investment in our example shows a positive cash flow:

Income	$10,000	
Less:	− 5,000	Total expenses
Cash flow	$ 5,000	

This $5,000 cash flow also passes through directly to the partners. For example, each may take 20 percent, or $1,000. And this $1,000 in cash to each partner is *tax-free* income. Remember, the investment shows a *loss,* and there is no tax on a loss.

In our example there were five partners and each shared equally in the profit and loss. This does not have to be the case, however. There can, for example, be a general partner who has a 50 percent share and 10 limited partners with 5 percent each. The division of loss and profit is now according to their participation in the partnership—50 percent to the general partner, 5 percent to each limited partner. A partnership can have any percentage of distribution. Some partners may receive 30 percent, others 1½ percent, and so on.

A-B distribution allows one partner to receive a paper loss while another receives cash flow.

It is not necessary that a partner participate in the cash flow and loss to the exact extent of participation in the partnership. It is possible to allocate all (or a percentage) of the loss to one partner and all (or a percentage) of the cash flow to another.

Let us go back to our syndicate investment example:

Income		$10,000
Less:		
Total expenses	$ 5,000	
Depreciation	10,000	−15,000
Paper loss		($ 5,000)

This property shows both a $5,000 paper loss and a $5,000 positive cash flow. In our original example we had five partners, each taking 20 percent of both cash flow and loss. Let us now, however, change the situation, for simplicity, to one where there are only two partners, A and B.

If A and B each have 50 percent of the partnership, their shares of the cash flow and loss on the property look like this:

A receives: $2,500   Positive cash flow
                 2,500   Paper loss

B receives: $2,500   Positive cash flow
                 2,500   Paper loss

It is possible, however, to change this allocation. One partner can receive all the cash flow and another all the loss. In such an allocation the distribution looks like this:

| A receives: | $5,000 Positive cash flow |
| B receives: | $5,000 Paper loss |

It is not necessary that a partner receive all loss or all cash flow. Any combination of percentages is possible. It is also not necessary that there be only two partners for this arrangement to work. Any number may participate, if the procedure is handled competently.

There is a problem with A-B distribution, and that has to do with IRS approval. If the IRS determines that the allocations are done strictly to avoid the payment of taxes, then the arrangement may be disallowed. It is frequently up to the partners to show that the allocation isn't done strictly to avoid taxes.

A typical use for an A-B distribution might be where partner A is over 65 years of age and has need of positive cash flow but, because he or she is retired and has no ordinary income, has no need of a tax shelter; while partner B may be just 35 years old and have a large income and a distinct need for a tax shelter.

A: 65 years old, retired, doesn't need tax shelter, needs income, receives $5,000 cash flow

B: 35 years old, has a high income, needs tax shelter, receives $5,000 paper loss

At-risk rules do not apply to syndicates in real estate.

Currently the at-risk rule applies to almost all types of investments *except* real estate. The at-risk rule, put simply, is that you cannot lose more than you invest. If the at-risk rule were to apply to real estate, it would look like Exhibit 18-1.

EXHIBIT 18-1 *Purchase of a $1 Million Investment Property*

	$200,000	Investment at risk
1st year loss (due to depreciation)	− 50,000	
	$150,000	Remaining investment at risk
2d year loss	− 50,000	
	$100,000	Remaining investment at risk
3d year loss	− 50,000	
	$ 50,000	Remaining investment at risk
4th year loss	− 50,000	
	-0-	Remaining investment at risk
		No longer deductible because loss now exceeds the
5th year loss	($ 50,000)	investment that was at risk

The *at-risk rule, however, does not apply to real estate investments.* It also does not apply to real estate investment in syndication. This probably is the single greatest benefit of investing in real estate and in particular of investing in a syndication as a limited partner. As a limited partner, you can receive a loss *in excess* of your original investment.

In our example, if there are five partners, each putting up $40,000 (a $200,000 investment) and each receiving 20 percent of the loss each year ($10,000), at the end of the fourth year each partner will have received in loss an amount equal to his total investment. The next year, however, because it is a real estate investment, each partner can continue to receive a loss, even though it is in excess of the investment at risk. There is *no limitation* on the amount of loss deductible.

5th year $50,000   Loss fully deductible (each partner receiving 20% or $10,000)

A newly formed partnership must adopt the calendar year for tax purposes unless a majority of its partners use a different fiscal period.

RECENT RULE CHANGES ON SYNDICATION

The rules for syndicating are fairly well established. Back in 1976, however, the Tax Reform Act of that year made two changes which are particularly significant to investors:

1. According to the 1976 Tax Reform Act, gain and loss must be divided on the basis of time participation in the partnership. For example, if a partnership has a $5,000 loss and there are two partners, A and B, and on July 1, 1979 (assuming they are on a calendar year), B sells his interest to C, here's how the loss for the year is divided:

$5,000 LOSS

A receives 50%, or $2,500
B receives 25%, or $1,250   (because B has been in the partnership for only half the year)
C receives 25%, or $1,250   (because C has been in the partnership for only half the year)

It is *not allowable* for B to sell in the middle of the year and still receive gain and loss for the full year with C not receiving gain and loss until the next year.

2. Fees are now limited. For partnerships starting after 1976, organizational fees must be capitalized and amortized over a 5-year period (or more). These expenses must be organizational in nature and incidental to the creation of the partnership. In addition, they should be the sort that are normally capitalized over the life of the partnership. (Note: Exceptions to this rule exist.)

208   *The Real Estate Agent's and Investor's Tax Book*

19

Business Deductions Real Estate Agents Can Take

While real estate agents do not receive preferential treatment from the government with regard to business deductions, the very nature of selling property gives them some unusually large deductions in relation to other businesses. It is the wise agent who finds out all the deductions to which he or she is entitled and then makes whatever preparations may be necessary in order to obtain them.

Business deductions are normally available only to individuals and companies actually engaged in a business. Since very many real estate agents are independent contractors, they fall within this group. If, however, an agent should be on a regular salary and be considered an employee rather than an independent contractor, many of these deductions may not apply. An agent in such a situation should check with an attorney or accountant for permissible employee deductions.

Real estate agents as independent contractors normally qualify for the following business deductions.

TELEPHONE

All telephone costs that are incurred as part of the agent's regular business are fully deductible. While this obviously includes a phone in a business office, it may also include calls made from an agent's home for a specific business purpose. To deduct such calls, however, the agent will probably need to note time and charges, person called, and reason for call (see "Entertainment Expenses" for other hints). A phone placed in the residence for business purposes when the agent has another regular place of business may or may not be deducted as a business expense; see the section on "Office at Home."

ADVERTISING

All business advertising expense that is paid to a media outlet or to an agency for procuring media space, as well as costs related to producing advertising, is normally deductible in full. This, however, does not necessarily include items which could be considered promotional in nature; see the section "Gifts." Political advertising is not deductible. Advertising in a political publication is not deductible.

CLOTHES

Clothes worn by the agent as part of his or her business are not normally deductible *unless* the clothes are peculiar to the business. For example, a dress or suit normally bought in any department store would not be deductible. A special jacket, hat, or item made specifically for the business in question (such as one which has a special color and shape and which has the business name placed on it in some manner) could be deductible. Simply buying a regular piece of clothing in a store and then sewing the business name on it probably does not make the entire piece of clothing deductible — only the cost of placing the business name on it.

GIFTS
Any gifts the agent gives to clients, business associates, or others at the end of the year or at any other time are limited to a maximum deduction of $25 per person. This does not include advertising or promotional gifts distributed generally. The limitation on these gifts is $4. If an employee is given an award, the usual deductible limit is $100.

ENTERTAINMENT EXPENSES
In general most entertainment expense is deductible as long as it bears a reasonable and proximate relation to a business activity. A notable exception is entertainment expense used to "drum up" business. This is not deductible.

The most common type of entertainment expense agents are likely to run into is meals. In general, these are deductible provided they are related to a business activity and adequate records are kept. The IRS usually insists that documentary evidence be kept for all meals over $25, but our experience has been that it is better to keep such evidence for all meals regardless of the cost. This tends to avoid later disputes with the IRS. (Reciprocal "treats"—I treat you today, you treat me tomorrow—are not deductible.)

The method of documenting meals that we have found to be particularly helpful is the following:

First, and of great importance, obtain and use a daily calendar. On the calendar mark the name of the client and the time and purpose of your meetings. When you take that client out for a meal, pay for the meal with a credit card, and on the receipt again note time and purpose. Finally, at the end of the day, attach the credit card receipt *directly to the calendar* at the point where the original notation was made (staple works fine here).

We have never seen the IRS question this method of documentation in an audit. On the other hand, when agents have kept receipts but not a calendar, we have frequently seen questions, and in many cases the expenses have been disallowed.

Extertainment Indirectly Related to Business
It may occur that a meeting will be scheduled with a lunch before and a dinner after. The question then arises whether the meals in such an

arrangement are deductible, even though no business was actually discussed during them. In general they are deductible, provided:

1. There is an actual conduct of business related to the entertainment expense at the meeting near the meal.
2. The entertainment expense occurs in a *clear business setting* (a hotel which provides meals and a conference room would probably be adequate).

TRAVEL EXPENSES
In general, an agent may deduct expenses for food and lodging while traveling on business, such as to lease or list property in a distant city. Expenses deducted can be for the full costs, but "lavish or extravagant" expenses may be disallowed. Records, including a calendar, must be kept for all travel expenses.

Taking a spouse along on a trip, such as to a convention in the United States, is deductible only if it can be shown that the spouse is *essential* to the *business purpose* of the trip. Trips to conventions in the United States for business purposes are generally deductible by agents; however, special rules apply should there be a convention outside the country. (Since in the normal course of business agents would not take convention trips outside the United States, our discussion does not cover this point. Check with an accountant or tax lawyer for the specific rules here.)

ENTERTAINMENT FACILITIES
Occasionally an agent will belong to a social or sports club with the primary purpose of membership being business. If the agent intends to entertain clients at the facility and to discuss items *directly related* to business, part of the dues of the club may be deducted, provided more than half (at least 51 percent) of the use is for business purposes. Such dues may be deducted only in proportion to directly related business use. For example, if club dues were $100 a month and an agent took clients there 50 percent of the time for purposes *directly related* to business, 20 percent of the time for purposes *associated with business,* 25 percent of the time for *pleasure,* and 5 percent of the time for *business meals,* the following would be true. Since more than half was business use (75 percent), a deduction is allowable. However, only that portion *directly related* to business may be deducted. That means that 50 percent plus 5 percent (business meals) could be deducted ($55 of the dues).

OFFICE AT HOME
In the past it was possible for an agent to work at a regular place of business and at the same time maintain an office at home. Expenses of

these home offices were deductible. For example, if the home were owned by the agent, expenses for that portion of the house used for business purposes, including interest, taxes, insurance, depreciation, maintenance, phone, utilities, and so on, were deductible. If a bedroom in a seven-room house were used for business work, one-seventh of the expenses for the entire home could be deducted.

The 1976 Tax Reform Act severely limited home office deductions, however. According to the reform act, deductions can be taken only if the office is a *principal place of business* or a *place where the agent meets with clients.* The agent must show that the office is set aside and that he or she *regularly and exclusively* uses it for business purposes.

Simply labeling a bedroom or a den an office will not do. The room may not be used for anything other than business purposes. It cannot be used for storage of items of personal use or as a spare bedroom when guests come. We have found that in order to avoid argument with the IRS it should be an entire room, rather than a portion of a room. The deduction is easier to claim if the office is a separate structure from the home.

REGULAR OFFICE RENT
The *rent* on a business office is deductible, as are other expenses, such as taxes, insurance, and maintenance, paid as part of the rent. If the business office is *owned* by the agent, normal deductions for investment property, such as property taxes, mortgage interest, insurance, utilities, and so on, may be taken (see Chapter 4 for more details).

OFFICE FURNITURE
If office furniture is leased, the full cost of the rental may be deducted. If it is purchased, the price should be capitalized over the useful life of the furniture (see the discussion below under "Automobiles" for additional details).

AUTOMOBILE
A real estate agent's greatest single expense can often be the automobile. There are several ways of treating this expense. For example, the car can be leased or it can be purchased outright. Cost of operation can be deducted on a standard "per mile" basis, or actual costs can be taken. We'll consider each of these deductions separately.

Auto Leasing versus Buying
There are several advantages to leasing an automobile, the biggest of which are probably leverage and convenience. Leverage is possible be-

cause in leasing frequently a security deposit is required which is much smaller than the down payment required when buying. Convenience occurs because frequently many leasing companies provide a complete maintenance program for their cars. In addition, they also may guarantee a turnover every few years, so that the agent can be assured of getting a new car at regular intervals.

From a tax viewpoint, all the costs of leasing, including a maintenance policy, are deductible for an agent as a business expense, provided the car is used 100 percent for business. This of necessity requires that an agent also have another car for personal use.

The rules for *use* of an automobile when a car is purchased are the same as for leasing. In buying, however, other tax advantages are available.

A 10 percent tax credit may be available on automobiles and furniture.

When one buys an automobile or furniture (whether new or used) for business purposes, an immediate 10 percent tax credit is available to the purchaser. This tax credit is in addition to any depreciation which may be claimed. It works in the following manner. If an agent buys a car, for example, costing $10,000, he or she may take up to 10 percent of the cost, in this case $1,000, as a credit off regular income tax. One of the requirements in order to qualify for the full credit is that the agent must hold the car for a minimum of 7 years. Since, in most cases, the actual holding period of a car is only about 3⅓ years, most agents probably will not get the full 10 percent credit. (For periods of 3 to 5 years, for example, only one-third of the 10 percent credit is allowed. If the full 10 percent is taken at the beginning of the holding period and the car is sold after 4 years, then two-thirds of the 10 percent will be recaptured. See the further discussion in Chapter 4.)

A 20 percent bonus depreciation may be available on automobile and furniture.

In the first year, subject to certain conditions discussed in Chapters 4 and 5, the agent may take a 20 percent one-time bonus depreciation on the car and furniture.

Declining-Balance Rates

In addition to other costs, the agent may depreciate new automobiles and furniture at a 200 percent declining-balance rate and used autos and furniture at 150 percent. (In order to get the full accelerated depreciation, it is suggested that the depreciation of the car be for 7 years. See Chapter 4 for a further discussion.)

Operating Expense Standard Deduction versus Actual Costs

The government allows a standard deduction of 18.5 cents a mile for the first 15,000 miles and 10 cents a mile for the balance as a standard deduction for operating expenses. If this deduction is taken, no other deduction for gas, repairs, and maintenance may be taken.

If the agent desires, instead of taking the standard deduction, the actual operating costs including gas, maintenance, and repairs may be taken each year.

Within a given year, only one method may be used. Between years, however, an agent may switch from standard to actual costs, or vice versa but *only* if the car is depreciated by the straight-line method. No switching is allowed if accelerated depreciation is used.

For an agent, the decision whether to use straight-line or accelerated depreciation can be a big one. For example, if the agent foresees large actual costs in one year and minimal costs in another, it might be better to use straight-line in order to be able to switch between the standard deduction and actual costs. This is often the case when the agent anticipates keeping the car a long time. Since repairs and maintenance tend to be minimal when the car is new and increase as the car gets older, an agent would presumably want the flexibility of going between standard deduction and actual costs.

It should be noted that large repairs to the car, such as replacing or rebuilding an engine or transmission, most likely would have to be capitalized and deducted over the entire life of the car. It is unlikely they could be expensed and deducted entirely in the year in which they occur.

EDUCATIONAL EXPENSES

The general rule is that educational expenses are deductible after the agent has met the minimum educational requirements to get into the profession, that is after he or she has been licensed. The educational costs involved in obtaining a license are not usually deductible.

Deductible costs include a wide variety of educational programs including refresher courses, seminars, and classes. Expenses related to these educational programs, such as transportation costs, lodging, and meals during programs held outside the agent's local area, may also be deductible.

OTHER DEDUCTIONS

In general, an agent can deduct any expense on a dollar-for-dollar basis which is *directly related* to business. We have tried to cover normal expenses. For unusual or unique expenses, however, an agent should check with an accountant or tax attorney.

Appendix I

Questions and Answers

Here are true-false, multiple choice, and essay questions that will help you check the knowledge you have gained from reading this book. After each answer, a page number is given. Since it is frequently very difficult, if not impossible, to sum up a tax concept within the framework of a question-and-answer format, the page numbers will allow the reader to refer back and see the context from which the question is drawn.

TRUE/FALSE

1. You have a total of 24 months to replace an old principal residence with a new one in order to claim a deferral of gain.   true/false

2. A taxpayer may always defer gain on the sale of a personal residence under the nonrecognition rule as long as the property in question is "residential."   true/false

3. A houseboat will qualify as a principal residence.   true/false

4. A new principal residence must cost more than an old one in order for any gain to be deferred.   true/false

5. If a principal residence is one unit of a five-unit apartment building, the owner is prohibited from deferring some of the gain upon the sale of the building.   true/false

6. It is allowable not to put any of the equity from an old principal residence into a new one and still defer the gain upon its sale.   true/false

7. The gain under the nonrecognition rule on the sale of a principal residence is permanently excluded from federal income tax.   true/false

8. Renting a principal residence out immediately prior to sale always results in the loss of the right to defer gain.   true/false

9. You can deduct from the sale price some of the costs of fixing up an old principal residence for the purpose of determining gain.   true/false

10. In a divorce, in some states, a husband retains all the benefits of the federal income tax rule of nonrecognition of gain on the sale of a principal residence.   true/false

11. It is possible to claim a tax loss on the sale of a principal residence.   true/false

12. You can deduct depreciation on a personal residence.   true/false

13. The cost of the commission on the sale of a principal residence can be deductible from ordinary income.   true/false

14. Property taxes and mortgage interest are deductible annually from personal income.   true/false

15. A tax shelter can be appropriately described as a paper loss.   true/false

16. Depreciation means, most simply, a loss in value from any cause.   true/false

17. When property is depreciated, no great distinction is made between land and improvements.   true/false

18. In real estate, you can lose more (on paper) than you invest.   true/false

19. A negative loss means a loss in excess of investment.   true/false

20. Interest frequently is the single largest expense on an investment property.   true/false

21. The greater the leverage in real estate, the better the investment always is.   true/false

22. A good tax shelter investment is one that is economically sound regardless of how small the write-off may be.   true/false

23. Only one year's worth of prepaid interest may be deducted as an investment expense.   true/false

24. All property taxes on investment real estate are fully deductible as expenses with regard to federal income tax.   true/false

25. It is possible to create a small, temporary tax shelter simply by paying property taxes in advance.   true/false

26. In general, all maintenance and repair work done to a piece of investment property is deductible against income.   true/false

27. In general, all improvements to investment property are deductible against investment income.   true/false

28. All construction-period interest and taxes may be deducted as they are paid.   true/false

29. For tax purposes, depreciation means the capitalization of an asset's value over a period of years.   true/false

30. The cash flow of a piece of property is influenced by depreciation.   true/false

31. It is possible to have both positive and negative cash flow on a piece of property at the same time.   true/false

32. When depreciation is calculated on improved real estate investment, the land can be depreciated.   true/false

33. The assessed valuation of a piece of property given by a local property taxing agency always is the best method to use in determining the value (basis) of a real estate improvement for income tax purposes.   true/false

34. It is sometimes advisable for buyer and seller to allocate the price paid for land and improvements separately.   true/false

35. Straight-line depreciation is considered the minimum rate.   true/false

36. A salvage value should be added when the declining-balance method of depreciation is used.   true/false

37. The graph of the declining-balance depreciation method has the appearance of straight-line.   true/false

38. It is necessary to recompute the amount to be depreciated for each year when the declining-balance method is used.   true/false

39. Both straight-line and declining-balance are forms of accelerated depreciation.   true/false

40. The minimum useful life term under the declining-balance method for residential property is 30 years.   true/false

41. Near the end of the depreciation term the annual deduction using the straight-line method will be greater than that of the declining-balance method.   true/false

42. When the component system of depreciation is used, it is necessary to give a separate useful life for the shell.   true/false

43. In the component system of depreciation, it is possible to use different useful lives for each component.   true/false

44. It is possible to get prior approval from the IRS on both the method and rate of depreciation used on a piece of property.   true/false

45. Depreciation transfers with ownership upon the sale of a piece of property.   true/false

46. IRS approval is required to switch from an accelerated method to a straight-line method of depreciation.   true/false

47. A sound real estate investment should be able to return positive cash flow before tax shelter considerations.   true/false

48. Once the cost (basis) of a real estate investment is established, it can never be lowered.   true/false

49. Gain on the sale of a real estate investment is determined by subtracting the original purchase price from the current selling price.   true/false

50. Capital gain in real estate is gain derived from the sale or exchange of investment property.   true/false

51. For the capital gains rule, investment property is defined as a piece of real estate used in trade or business and held for the production of income.   true/false

52. A dealer in real estate cannot take advantage of the capital gains treatment of real property.   true/false

53. A taxpayer generally may not claim as a capital gain that portion of gain which is due to accelerated depreciation.   true/false

54. In certain cases, recapture of depreciation or a portion of it may be forgiven. true/false

55. "Gain realized" is that part of the recognized gain the government realizes for tax purposes. true/false

56. A four-cornered exchange is the largest exchange legally possible. true/false

57. An investor's tax-free exchange usually involves three or more parties. true/false

58. In a tax-free exchange there must be a trade of properties. true/false

59. In a tax-free exchange the property to be exchanged must be held for productive use in trade or business or for investment. true/false

60. A dealer may make only five tax-free exchanges per year. true/false

61. Unimproved real property may not normally be exchanged tax-free for improved real property. true/false

62. A lease for over 30 years is normally considered the same as fee title or as real property. true/false

63. All "boot" in a tax-free exchange is taxable. true/false

64. In a tax-free exchange a nonqualifying property is simply an item which does not incur a tax liability. true/false

65. Boot is normally considered "qualifying property." true/false

66. Any boot in a tax-free exchange automatically denies tax-free status to the entire transaction. true/false

67. In a tax-free exchange mortgages assumed are considered boot to person relieved of liability. true/false

68. In a tax-free exchange taking a mortgage "subject to" eliminates it from consideration as boot. true/false

69. For tax purposes, a tax-free exchange is optional, depending on the desires of the taxpayer. true/false

70. No loss may be recognized on a tax-free exchange. true/false

71. When boot exceeds gain realized on a tax-free exchange, the excess boot reduces the basis of the original property. true/false

72. A "clean" tax-free exchange keeps the exchange portion of the transaction separate from the cash part. true/false

73. Simultaneous closing of all escrows is not a necessary part of all tax-free exchanges. true/false

74. In a "Type II" exchange, the purchase-sale occurs first, the trade second. true/false

75. The capital gains holding period continues through a tax-free exchange. true/false

76. Any cash received by the taxpayer desiring tax-free status in an exchange may be considered boot. true/false

77. One method sometimes used to avoid the receipt of boot in a tax-free exchange is the use of a second mortgage to balance equities. true/false

78. Refinancing prior to an exchange can sometimes avoid problems with boot. true/false

79. Keeping title clear and separate during a tax-free exchange is usually considered desirable. true/false

80. A "step-sale" is a frequently used type of tax-free exchange created specifically to meet IRS requirements. true/false

81. Recapture of depreciation cannot become a problem in a tax-free exchange. true/false

82. In an "agent's exchange," the agent participates as a principal. true/false

83. In a "Type II' tax-free exchange the agent typically represents the buyer instead of the taxpayer. true/false

84. In a tax-free exchange, the tax is not excluded, only deferred until a later date. true/false

85. The mortgage a taxpayer is relieved of is offset by the mortgage assumed in a tax-free exchange. true/false

86. In a tax-free exchange, recognized gain is equal to boot up to the extent of the gain realized. true/false

87. In a tax-free exchange boot is equal to cash minus personalty. true/false

88. In a tax-free exchange, realized gain is equal to property received plus cash plus liability relieved minus adjusted basis of property given minus liability assumed. true/false

89. A car would always be considered boot in a real estate tax-free exchange. true/false

90. In a foreclosure, for tax purposes, the mortgage balance is considered the equivalent of the sale price. true/false

91. An installment sale can be used to reduce the taxes on the sale of a piece of real estate.   true/false

92. In an installment sale the seller must receive no more than 29 percent of the selling price in the year of sale.   true/false

93. The selling price in an installment sale includes cash, mortgages, and personalty,   true/false

94. Commission and selling expenses reduce the sale price for calculating the maximum down payment in an installment sale.   true/false

95. Payments in an installment sale must be made in three or more installments and must cover at least 2 years.   true/false

96. The down payment in the year of sale in an installment sale does not include new mortgages given by the seller.   true/false

97. The "contract price" in an installment sale is the total amount of all payments to be received by the seller.   true/false

98. In an installment sale taxable income due to accelerated depreciation is reported first. Only then can capital gains income be reported.   true/false

99. It is possible to have an installment sale in which there are only two payments and the two payments are only one week or less apart.   true/false

100. Dealers in real estate may not use the installment sale method of selling.   true/false

101. A deferred-payment sale frequently may be used where an installment sale cannot be used.   true/false

102. In a deferred-payment sale it is helpful if the buyer pays all cash and there is no mortgage involved.   true/false

103. In a deferred-payment sale the difference between the fair market value of a mortgage and the face value may be reported as gain only if and when it is actually collected.   true/false

104. In a deferred-payment sale the difference between face value and fair market value of a mortgage may be reported as capital gains when received.   true/false

105. Most vacation homes can be used as tax shelters.   true/false

106. A vacation home can be a house or a condominium, but it may not be an apartment or a boat.   true/false

107. In general, if a taxpayer personally uses a vacation home for more than 14 days a year, or for 10 percent or more of the time rented, whichever is greater, no tax shelter may be claimed on the property.   true/false

108. When expenses are calculated on a vacation home used also largely as a personal residence, deductions for maintenance, utilities, and advertising must be made before a deduction for depreciation is allowed.   true/false

109. If an investor rents out a vacation home for 14 days or less a year, the taxpayer need not declare the rent received as income.   true/false

110. Under the "hobby rules" the taxpayer must establish that a piece of property was used for investment and not pleasure purposes in order to claim business deductions on it.   true/false

111. If a taxpayer agrees to trade the use of a vacation home for a week with another vacation home owner under an agreement that provides each party pay full rental, it is presumed to be personal use by both parties for tax purposes.   true/false

112. A taxpayer receiving an option on a piece of property does not normally have to report the option money as income until the option is exercised or forfeited, even if it is in a later tax year.   true/false

113. When an option is exercised, for the optionee, the holding period for capital gains treatment on the property begins the day following the exercise of the option.   true/false

114. An option for more than a year that is not exercised can only be reported as a long-term loss by the optionee.   true/false

115. One danger with a large option is that the IRS might interpret it as a sale of the property with an agreement to pay the remainder of the purchase price at a later date.   true/false

116. The major tax advantage of the wraparound today is to allow the purchaser to make a substantial prepayment of interest.   true/false

117. Advance rental payments are not treated as taxable income until the last month of the lease.   true/false

118. Advance rental payments may be deducted by a tenant as soon as they are paid.   true/false

119. For cash-basis taxpayers, security deposits are normally considered as taxable income as soon as received.　　true/false

120. For a lessee, a lease bonus may be deducted as soon as paid.　　true/false

121. For a lessor, a lease bonus must be counted as taxable income as soon as received.　　true/false

122. An agent's fee for negotiating a lease normally may be deducted immediately as soon as paid.　　true/false

123. In a contract sale, both buyer and seller may not deduct the same expenses, although both separately may be entitled to do so.　　true/false

124. In a limited partnership there must be at least one general partner who has unlimited liability.　　true/false

125. The number of partners in a real estate syndicate may be determined by both federal and state law.　　true/false

126. A-B distributions in limited partnerships are not allowed.　　true/false

127. A-B distributions allow one partner to receive a paper loss while another receives positive cash flow.　　true/false

128. The at-risk rules apply to limited partnerships.　　true/false

129. In order to claim an office in the home as a deduction, a real estate agent must only show that the office is a principal place of business or a place where the agent meets with clients.　　true/false

130. It is always to the agent's advantage, from a tax viewpoint, to lease an automobile rather than to buy it.　　true/false

131. A 20 percent bonus depreciation deduction may be available to agents on both auto and furniture purchases.　　true/false

132. The government allows a standard deduction of 18.5 cents a mile for the first 15,000 miles for business use of a car.　　true/false

133. An agent may switch from the standard deduction to actual costs from year to year as long as an accelerated method of depreciation is used.　　true/false

TRUE/FALSE ANSWERS

1. false (7)	34. true (65)	67. true (116)	100. false (177)
2. false (9)	35. true (66)	68. false (116)	101. true (177)
3. true (9)	36. false (67)	69. false (117)	102. false (177)
4. false (10)	37. false (72)	70. true (117)	103. true (178)
5. false (13)	38. true (68)	71. true (131)	104. false (178)
6. true (11)	39. false (67)	72. true (133)	105. false (152)
7. false (11)	40. false (73)	73. true (133)	106. false (153)
8. false (13)	41. true (72)	74. false (134)	107. true (153)
9. true (17)	42. true (73)	75. true (135)	108. true (154)
10. false (19)	43. true (73)	76. true (138)	109. true (155)
11. false (27)	44. true (74)	77. true (138)	110. true (155)
12. false (30)	45. false (75)	78. true (137)	111. true (157)
13. false (21)	46. false (76)	79. true (140)	112. true (160)
14. true (29)	47. true (87)	80. false (142)	113. true (161)
15. true (34)	48. false (90)	81. false (143)	114. true (162)
16. true (35)	49. false (91)	82. true (145)	115. true (162)
17. false (35)	50. true (92)	83. false (148)	116. false (163)
18. true (37)	51. false (93)	84. true (153)	117. false (164)
19. true (37)	52. true (93)	85. true (154)	118. false (164)
20. true (39)	53. true (96)	86. true (154)	119. true (164)
21. false (39)	54. true (99)	87. false (154)	120. false (165)
22. true (42)	55. false (107)	88. true (154)	121. true (165)
23. false (46)	56. false (110)	89. true (153)	122. false (166)
24. true (47)	57. true (111)	90. true (162)	123. true (169)
25. true (47)	58. true (113)	91. true (166)	124. true (173)
26. true (47)	59. true (113)	92. false (167)	125. true (174)
27. false (48)	60. false (114)	93. true (168)	126. false (176)
28. false (52)	61. false (114)	94. false (168)	127. true (177)
29. true (60)	62. true (115)	95. false (169)	128. true (177)
30. false (62)	63. true (116)	96. true (169)	129. false (182)
31. false (62)	64. false (116)	97. true (172)	130. false (183)
32. false (63)	65. false (116)	98. true (175)	131. true (184)
33. false (64)	66. false (116)	99. true (176)	132. true (185)
			133. false (185)

MULTIPLE CHOICE

1. The total number of months allowable during which a new principal residence may replace an old one (including the time before the sale of the old one and the time for any new construction) in order to claim a deferral of gain is:
   - *a.* 18
   - *b.* 24
   - *c.* 36
   - *d.* 42
   - *e.* 48

2. Which, if any, of the following are *not* normally a deductible expense on investment property?
   a. Mileage from the owner's house to the property and back
   b. Utilities for the property
   c. Management fees
   d. Gardening costs
   e. Telephone costs

3. Which of the following is normally not considered investment income?
   a. Rental income
   b. Mortgage income
   c. Occupational income

4. Which of the following declining-balance depreciation rates is *not* commonly used?
   a. 125 percent
   b. 150 percent
   c. 175 percent
   d. 200 percent

5. The capital gains holding period for real estate is which of the following:
   a. 6 months
   b. 9 months
   c. 1 year

6. Which of the following is *not* true of a tax-free exchange?
   a. It may not be used for a principal residence.
   b. There is a maximum 42-month waiting period.
   c. Property must be traded.

7. Which of the following is *not* true of a deferral of gain on the sale of a principal residence?
   a. It may be sold for cash.
   b. It may be used on property held for investment.
   c. Property must be replaced by other property.

8. Which of the following is *not* a common reason given for using a tax-free exchange?
   a. It allows for obtaining better-leveraged property.
   b. An agent may make two commissions instead of one.
   c. It reduces the gain realized on a sale.
   d. It solves the problem of obtaining financing in a tight market.

9. Which, if any, of the following business deductions may a real estate agent
   normally *not* take?
   a. Telephone
   b. Advertising
   c. Clothes (not uniform)
   d. Gifts
   e. Entertainment

MULTIPLE CHOICE ANSWERS

1. *d*	(7)	4. *c*	(70)	7. *b*	(177)
2. none	(46–50)	5. *c*	(94)	8. *c*	(108)
3. *c*	(57)	6. *b*	(108)	9. *c*	(180)

ESSAY QUESTIONS

1. QUESTION: How do I determine the adjusted basis when calculating gain
   on the sale of a principal residence?
   ANSWER: Adjusted basis is the original cost of the old residence plus the
   cost of improvements to the property during your period of ownership.   (10)

2. QUESTION: Why can't I simply buy and sell as many principal residences as
   I want over any time period and defer the gain on all of them?
   ANSWER: The IRS rule is specific. No more than one principal residence
   every 18 months may have its gain on sale deferred.   (15)

3. QUESTION: How can I increase the cost of my new personal residence even
   after I purchase it in order to comply with the deferral of gain rules?
   ANSWER: The cost may be increased by improving the property by adding,
   for example, a new room or a swimming pool. These improvements, however, must be within the 18-month (up to 24-month for new construction)
   time limit for the rule.   (17)

4. QUESTION: How may I defer the gain on the sale of my principal residence
   if I sell by the installment method?
   ANSWER: The gain on an installment sale may be deferred. The ratio of
   gain to the total amount of installments is determined and that ratio is
   applied to determine what part of each payment is recognized gain and what
   part is deferred.   (19)

5. QUESTION: How does the IRS know what I'm doing regarding the sale and
   purchase of my principal residence?
   ANSWER: Each taxpayer must report the sale of a principal residence in
   order to claim a deferral of gain. Reports of subsequent purchase of a new
   principal residence (or of failure to purchase within the time limit) must also
   be made.   (22)

6. QUESTION: Is there any way I can reduce the gain on the sale of my principal
   residence?

ANSWER: One method is to keep track of all improvements made to the property. These are added to the cost to form the adjusted basis. The higher the basis, the lower the gain. (17)

7. QUESTION: How is a real estate tax shelter created?
ANSWER: A tax shelter is created when a piece of property shows a loss on paper greater than its income. This excess loss is then used to offset or "shelter" the owner's regular income. (34)

8. QUESTION: How does a piece of property show a loss on paper?
ANSWER: All allowable expenses on real estate, except for depreciation, are deductible on a dollar-for-dollar basis. Depreciation, however, is deductible even though no money on the part of the taxpayer has actually been spent. Depreciation, therefore, is a loss that occurs principally on paper. (35)

9. QUESTION: What is a bad tax shelter?
ANSWER: A bad tax shelter is one in which the mixture of investment, income and expenses is distorted so that there is negative cash flow. (37)

10 QUESTION: Over what period of time is the cost of an improvement, such as a swimming pool, written off on investment property?
ANSWER: The cost is depreciated over the estimated useful life of the improvement. (48)

11. QUESTION: How do I determine whether an item is considered repair and maintenance or an improvement?
ANSWER: There are no specific rules that can be followed in all cases. The taxpayer, however, must be able to satisfy the government that a decision to consider an item a repair, and not an improvement, has merit sufficient to justify its being immediately expensed. (49)

12. QUESTION: When is bonus depreciation on personal property available on real estate investments
ANSWER: It is a one-time special depreciation of 20 percent of the value which may be taken at the time of purchase, subject to several conditions. See Chapter 4 for details. (77)

13. QUESTION: Are expenses on an investment property immediately deductible from regular income?
ANSWER: No. Investment expenses must first be offset by investment income. Only then may any resulting loss be deducted from regular income. (58)

14. QUESTION: Why isn't negative cash flow affected by depreciation?
ANSWER: Negative cash flow is money that the taxpayer must take out of pocket and put into a property to support it (as opposed to positive cash flow in which the property pays money to the taxpayer). The calculation for cash flow is made on the basis of operating income versus operating expenses and therefore is made before the calculation for depreciation. It is true, however, that a large amount of depreciation can result in a tax shelter, which, for individuals in higher tax brackets, may result in tax savings that overtake and even surpass a negative cash flow. (62)

15. QUESTION: How is the basis of a real estate investment affected by depreciation?
ANSWER: Depreciation lowers the basis. In the calculation all the depreciation claimed during the entire period of ownership is added together and that total amount is subtracted from the original basis or cost of the property. (63)

16. QUESTION: How is gain affected by depreciation?
ANSWER: Since all depreciation must be subtracted from the original basis before gain is calculated, depreciation always increases gain. The greater the depreciation on a piece of property, the greater the potential gain upon sale. (90)

17. QUESTION: Prior to October 31, 1978, how did the alternate method of figuring capital gains work?
ANSWER: The maximum tax was limited to 25 percent of the first $50,000 gain and 35 percent on any gain over $50,000.

18. QUESTION: How does the regular method of figuring capital gains work?
ANSWER: It works quite simply. After the total capital gain is calculated, 60 percent of that figure is excluded, and the other 40 percent is added to the taxpayer's regular income. (94)

19. QUESTION: How do I determine what portion of my gain was due to an accelerated method of depreciation?
ANSWER: First calculate the total depreciation if only a straight-line method was used. Next subtract this straight-line method amount from the actual amount of depreciation claimed. Any portion in excess of the straight-line method was due to an accelerated method of depreciation. (96)

20. QUESTION: How can I keep "gain realized" and "gain recognized" straight?
ANSWER: It's quite simple. "Gain realized" means how much gain you actually received or realized yourself. "Gain recognized" means how much of that gain realized is recognized by the government for tax purposes. (107)

21. QUESTION: What does "realty for realty and personalty for personalty" mean?
ANSWER: In order to have a tax-free exchange, the properties being traded must qualify under IRS rules. In general, a piece of real property may be traded tax-free for another piece of real estate (provided all other requirements are met). But a piece of real estate may not be traded tax-free for a piece of personal property, such as a boat. (114)

22. QUESTION: Are there any types of property specifically excluded from a tax-free exchange?
ANSWER: Yes. They include stock in trade or other property held primarily for sale, stocks, bonds, notes, choses in action, certificates of trust or beneficial action, or other securities or evidences of indebtedness or interest. (116)

23. QUESTION: What's the difference between basis and equity?
ANSWER: Equity is current value less mortgages—your interest in the property. Basis is the cost of the property plus improvements less depreciation (if any). Equity is used when the owner's interest in the property is calculated. Basis is used when the owner's gain or tax liability is calculated. (128)

24. QUESTION: What is one of the biggest dangers of the "agent's exchange?"
ANSWER: It is that the agent will be construed by the IRS as an agent and not as a principal. The result of this is that the taxpayer may lose tax-free status. (148)

25. QUESTION: How can refinancing a piece of property prior to an installment sale potentially affect the tax status of the sale itself?
ANSWER: If the refinanced mortgage is higher than the seller's basis in the property, the excess is included in the down payment for purposes of computing an installment sale. If not taken into account, this could have the effect of driving the first installment above the 30 percent limitation and depriving the transaction of installment sale status. (171)

26. QUESTION: In an installment sale, how do I know which portion of each payment is taxable and which portion is tax free?
ANSWER: The taxable portion of each payment is found by obtaining the percentage determined by dividing the contract price into the gain. That percentage of each payment is taxable. The remaining amount is nontaxable. (173)

27. QUESTION: In its simplest sense, how is business lease money handled for tax purposes?
ANSWER: In general, the tenant may deduct lease money as an expense as soon as it is paid. The landlord must count the lease money as income as soon as it is received. (163)

28. QUESTION: What are the tax advantages of joining a limited partnership in a real estate investment?
ANSWER: There are many advantages, including the following: (1) A limited partner will normally not be classified as a dealer no matter how many limited partnerships he or she may enter; (2) "pass-through" benefits allow limited partners to take advantage of both paper losses and positive cash flows; and (3) the limited partner's liability is limited in many cases to the original investment. (173)

Appendix II

Depreciation Tables

These tables have been formulated to give you, quickly and easily, the actual depreciation figures for your property. They allow you to determine, with simple calculations, the depreciation in a given year, the cumulative depreciation up to that year, and the undepreciated balance. The tables show the yearly depreciation for the first years; thereafter they show depreciation at 5-year intervals. (For a discussion of depreciation, check Chapter 5.)

LOOKING AT THE TABLES

There are four tables (one each for lives of twenty, twenty-five, thirty and forty years). The tables are divided in sections, each section giving different rates of depreciation: straight-line and 125 percent, 150 percent, and 200 percent declining-balance. (See Chapter 5 for rules on allowable rates and terms for different properties.) Under each rate of depreciation there are five columns: the first column indicates the year; column 2 gives the annual percentage of depreciation which may be taken for that year under the method and rate being used; column 3 gives the cumulative percentage of depreciation taken through that year; column 4 gives the depreciation that would be taken if the property in question had an adjusted basis of $100,000; column 5 is the remaining undepreciated balance for the $100,000 sample property given in column 4.

HOW TO USE THE TABLES

Column 1 gives the year of depreciation. Let us say you have a property with an adjusted basis of $50,000. You have determined that you are going to depreciate that property for a term of 20 years at a rate of 125 percent. You now want to know what the first year's depreciation will be. Turn to Table A-1, Section 2, and read down the first column to year 1. Immediately to its right, in column 2, is the annual percentage to apply to the original adjusted basis to determine that year's depreciation. The number is 6.25. Now simply multiply the original adjusted basis of your property, $50,000, by 6.25 percent. This yields $3,125, which is the first year's depreciation.

Let us say that now you want to know the depreciation under the same life and rate for year 5 instead of year 1. Simply go down the first column to year 5 and read across to column 2. The percentage of original adjusted basis is now 4.83. Multiply 4.83 times $50,000: the depreciation for year 5 is $2,415. If you now want to know the total depreciation taken under this rate and term for this property up to year 5, simply go to column 3. The cumulative depreciation is shown here, again expressed as a percentage of the original adjusted basis. Multiply the number shown for year 5 (27.58%) by the original adjusted basis, $50,000, and you learn that the total depreciation taken by year 5 is $13,790. To find the amount yet to be depreciated, simply take the total depreciation (in this case at year 5 we have found it is $13,790) and subtract from the original adjusted basis of $50,000:

Cost basis	$50,000
Accumulated depreciation	13,790
Adjusted cost basis	$36,210

At year 5, the undepreciated balance (adjusted cost basis) is $36,210.

As a guide, columns 4 and 5 have been provided. These assume a property with a $100,000 adjusted basis. In column 4, for each life and rate, the annual depreciation has been calculated for the specimen $100,000 piece of property. In addition, column 5 shows the undepreciated balance (adjusted basis) for our $100,000 piece of property.

To determine the annual depreciation at year 5 for a 20-year life at 125 percent for our specimen $100,000 adjusted-basis property, simply go to Table A-1, Section 2, year 5, and read across to column 4. The actual amount is given: $4,828. To find the undepreciated balance remaining (adjusted basis) at year 5, read across to column 5: $72,420.

ALTERNATE METHOD

An alternate method of using these charts is to calculate the figures desired using only multiples of columns 4 and 5. For example, if your property has an adjusted basis of only $10,000 instead of the $100,000 given in our specimen, you could still use the figures in columns 4 and 5 directly. Simply find the appropriate life, rate, and year — read across — and then move the decimal one place to the left. If your property were worth $1 million instead of $100,000, the same process could be repeated by moving the decimal point one place to the right. And so on. The tables follow.

TABLE A-1, Section 1   Depreciation over 20 Years. Straight-Line

Year	Annual percent	Cumulative percent	Annual allowance	Adjusted basis
1	5.00	5.00	$5,000	$95,000
2	5.00	10.00	5,000	90,000
3	5.00	15.00	5,000	85,000
4	5.00	20.00	5,000	80,000
5	5.00	25.00	5,000	75,000
6	5.00	30.00	5,000	70,000
7	5.00	35.00	5,000	65,000
8	5.00	40.00	5,000	60,000
9	5.00	45.00	5,000	55,000
10	5.00	50.00	5,000	50,000
15	5.00	75.00	5,000	25,000
20	5.00	100.00	5,000	0

TABLE A-1, Section 2   Depreciation over 20 Years, 125 Percent Declining-Balance

Year	Annual	Cumulative percent	Annual allowance	Adjusted basis
1	6.25	6.25	$6,250	$93,750
2	5.86	12.11	5,859	87,891
3	5.49	17.60	5,493	82,398
4	5.15	22.75	5,150	77,248
5	4.83	27.58	4,828	72,420
6	4.53	32.11	4,526	67,894
7	4.24	36.35	4,243	63,651
8	3.98	40.33	3,978	59,673
9	3.73	44.06	3,730	55,943
10	3.50	47.55	3,496	52,447
15	2.53	62.02	2,532	37,982
20	1.81	72.86	1,810	27,142

TABLE A-1, Section 3   Depreciation over 20 Years, 150 Percent Declining-Balance

Year	Annual percent	Cumulative percent	Annual allowance	Adjusted basis
1	7.50	7.50	$7.500	$92,500
2	6.94	14.44	6,938	85,562
3	6.42	20.85	6,417	79,145
4	5.94	26.79	5,936	73,209
5	5.49	32.28	5,491	67,718
6	5.08	37.36	5,079	62,639
7	4.70	42.06	4,698	57,941
8	4.35	46.40	4,346	53,595
9	4.02	50.42	4,020	49,575
10	3.72	54.14	3,718	45,857
15	2.52	68.95	2,518	31,054
20	1.71	78.97	1,705	21,030

TABLE A-1, Section 4   Depreciation over 20 Years, 200 Percent Declining-Balance

Year	Annual percent	Cumulative percent	Annual allowance	Adjusted basis
1	10.00	10.00	$10,000	$90,000
2	9.00	19.00	9,000	81,000
3	8.10	27.10	8,100	72,900
4	7.29	34.39	7,290	65,610
5	6.56	40.95	6,561	59,049
6	5.90	46.86	5,905	53,144
7	5.31	52.17	5,314	47,830
8	4.78	56.95	4,783	43,047
9	4.30	61.26	4,305	38,742
10	3.87	65.13	3,874	34,868
15	2.29	79.41	2,288	20,589
20	1.35	87.84	1,351	12,157

TABLE A-2, Section 1   Depreciation over 25 Years, Straight-Line

Year	Annual percent	Cumulative percent	Annual allowance	Adjusted basis
1	4.00	4.00	$4,000	$96,000
2	4.00	8.00	4,000	92,000
3	4.00	12.00	4,000	88,000
4	4.00	16.00	4,000	84,000
5	4.00	20.00	4,000	80,000
6	4.00	24.00	4,000	76,000
7	4.00	28.00	4,000	72,000
8	4.00	32.00	4,000	68,000
9	4.00	36.00	4,000	64,000
10	4.00	40.00	4,000	60,000
15	4.00	60.00	4,000	40,000
20	4.00	80.00	4,000	20,000
25	4.00	100.00	4,000	0

TABLE A-2, Section 2   Depreciation over 25 Years, 125 Percent Declining-Balance

Year	Annual percent	Cumulative percent	Annual allowance	Adjusted basis
1	5.00	5.00	$5,000	$95,000
2	4.75	9.75	4,750	90,250
3	4.51	14.26	4,512	85,738
4	4.29	18.55	4,287	81,451
5	4.07	22.62	4,073	77,378
6	3.87	26.49	3,869	73,509
7	3.68	30.17	3,675	69,834
8	3.49	33.66	3,492	66,342
9	3.32	36.98	3,317	63,025
10	3.15	40.13	3,151	59,874
15	2.44	53.67	2,438	46,329
20	1.89	64.15	1,887	35,848
25	1.46	72.26	1,460	27,738

TABLE A-2, Section 3 Depreciation over 25 Years, 150 Percent Declining-Balance

Year	Annual percent	Cumulative percent	Annual allowance	Adjusted basis
1	6.00	6.00	$6,000	$94,000
2	5.64	11.64	5,640	88,360
3	5.30	16.94	5,302	83,058
4	4.98	21.93	4,983	78,075
5	4.68	26.61	4,685	73,390
6	4.40	31.01	4,403	68,987
7	4.14	35.15	4,139	64,848
8	3.89	39.04	3,891	60,957
9	3.66	42.70	3,657	57,300
10	3.44	46.14	3,438	53,862
15	2.52	60.47	2,523	39,529
20	1.85	70.99	1,852	29,010
25	1.36	78.71	1,359	21,290

TABLE A-2, Section 4 Depreciation over 25 Years, 200 Percent Declining-Balance

Year	Annual percent	Cumulative percent	Annual allowance	Adjusted basis
1	8.00	8.00	$8,000	$92,000
2	7.36	15.36	7,360	84,640
3	6.77	22.13	6,771	77,869
4	6.23	28.36	6,230	71,639
5	5.73	34.09	5,731	65,908
6	5.27	39.36	5,273	60,635
7	4.85	44.22	4,851	55,784
8	4.46	48.68	4,463	51,321
9	4.11	52.78	4,106	47,215
10	3.78	56.56	3,777	43,438
15	2.49	71.37	2,490	28,629
20	1.64	81.13	1,640	18,870
25	1.08	87.56	1,081	12,437

TABLE A-3, Section 1   Depreciation over 30 Years, Straight-Line

Year	Annual percent	Cumulative percent	Annual allowance	Adjusted basis
1	3.33	3.33	$3,333	$96,667
2	3.33	6.67	3,334	93,333
3	3.33	10.00	3,333	90,000
4	3.33	13.33	3,333	86,667
5	3.33	16.67	3,334	83,333
6	3.33	20.00	3,333	80,000
7	3.33	23.33	3,333	76,667
8	3.33	26.67	3,334	73,333
9	3.33	30.00	3,333	70,000
10	3.33	33.33	3,333	66,667
15	3.33	50.00	3,333	50,000
20	3.33	66.67	3,334	33,333
25	3.33	83.33	3,333	16,667
30	3.33	100.00	3,333	0

TABLE A-3, Section 2   Depreciation over 30 Years, 125 Percent Declining-Balance

Year	Annual percent	Cumulative percent	Annual allowance	Adjusted basis
1	4.17	4.17	$4,170	$95,830
2	4.00	8.17	3,996	91,834
3	3.83	12.00	3,829	88,005
4	3.67	15.67	3,670	84,335
5	3.52	19.19	3,517	80,818
6	3.37	22.56	3,370	77,448
7	3.23	25.79	3,230	74,218
8	3.09	28.88	3,095	71,123
9	2.97	31.85	2,966	68,157
10	2.84	34.69	2,842	65,315
15	2.30	47.22	2,297	52,786
20	1.85	57.34	1,856	42,662
25	1.50	65.52	1,500	34,478
30	1.21	72.14	1,213	27,864

TABLE A-3, Section 3   Depreciation over 30 Years, 150 Percent Declining-Balance

Year	Annual percent	Cumulative percent	Annual allowance	Adjusted basis
1	5.00	5.00	$5,000	$95,000
2	4.75	9.75	4,750	90,250
3	4.51	14.26	4,512	85,738
4	4.29	18.55	4,287	81,451
5	4.07	22.62	4,073	77,378
6	3.87	26.49	3,869	73,509
7	3.68	30.17	3,675	69,834
8	3.49	33.66	3,492	66,342
9	3.32	36.98	3,317	63,025
10	3.15	40.13	3,151	59,874
15	2.44	53.67	2,438	46,329
20	1.89	64.15	1,887	35,848
25	1.46	72.26	1,460	27,738
30	1.13	78.54	1,130	21,462

TABLE A-3, Section 4   Depreciation over 30 Years, 200 Percent Declining-Balance

Year	Annual percent	Cumulative percent	Annual allowance	Adjusted basis
1	6.67	6.67	$6,670	$93,330
2	6.22	12.89	6,225	87,105
3	5.81	18.70	5,810	81,295
4	5.42	24.12	5,422	75,873
5	5.06	29.18	5,061	70,812
6	4.72	33.90	4,723	66,089
7	4.41	38.31	4,408	61,681
8	4.12	42.43	4,114	57,567
9	3.84	46.27	3,840	53,727
10	3.58	49.85	3,584	50,143
15	2.54	64.48	2,538	35,507
20	1.80	74.85	1,797	25,144
25	1.27	82.19	1,273	19,078
30	0.90	87.39	901	12,609

TABLE A-4, Section 1   Depreciation over 40 Years, Straight-Line

Year	Annual percent	Cumulative percent	Annual allowance	Adjusted basis
1	2.50	2.50	$2,500	$97,500
2	2.50	5.00	2,500	95,000
3	2.50	7.50	2,500	92,500
4	2.50	10.00	2,500	90,000
5	2.50	12.50	2,500	87,500
6	2.50	15.00	2,500	85,00C
7	2.50	17.50	2,500	82,500
8	2.50	20.00	2,500	80,000
9	2.50	22.50	2,500	77,500
10	2.50	25.00	2,500	75,000
15	2.50	37.50	2,500	62,500
20	2.50	50.00	2,500	50,000
25	2.50	62.50	2,500	37,500
30	2.50	75.00	2,500	25,000
35	2.50	87.50	2,500	12,500
40	2.50	100.00	2,500	0

TABLE A-4, Section 2   Depreciation over 40 Years, 125 Percent Declining-Balance

Year	Annual percent	Cumulative percent	Annual allowance	Adjusted basis
1	3.12	3.12	$3,120	$96,880
2	3.02	6.14	3,023	93,857
3	2.93	9.07	2,928	90,929
4	2.84	11.91	2,837	88,092
5	2.75	14.66	2,748	85,343
6	2.66	17.32	2,663	82,681
7	2.58	19.90	2,580	80,101
8	2.50	22.40	2,499	77,602
9	2.42	24.82	2,421	75,181
10	2.35	27.17	2,346	72,835
15	2.00	37.84	2,002	62,160
20	1.71	46.95	1,708	53,050
25	1.46	54.72	1,458	45,274
30	1.24	61.34	1,244	38,639
35	1.06	67.00	1,062	32,976
40	0.91	71.86	906	28,144

TABLE A-4, Section 3   Depreciation over 40 Years, 150 Percent Declining-Balance

Year	Annual percent	Cumulative percent	Annual allowance	Adjusted basis
1	3.75	3.75	$3,750	$96,250
2	3.61	7.36	3,609	92,641
3	3.47	10.83	3,474	89,167
4	3.34	14.18	3,344	85,823
5	3.22	17.40	3,218	82,605
6	3.10	20.49	3,098	79,507
7	2.98	23.47	2,982	76,525
8	2.87	26.34	2,870	73,655
9	2.76	29.11	2,762	70,893
10	2.66	31.76	2,658	68,235
15	2.20	43.63	2,196	56,365
20	1.81	53.44	1,814	46,560
25	1.50	61.54	1,498	38,461
30	1.24	68.23	1,238	31,771
35	1.02	73.76	1,023	26,244
40	0.85	78.32	845	21,678

TABLE A-4, Section 4   Depreciation over 40 Years, 200 Percent Declining-Balance

Year	Annual percent	Cumulative percent	Annual allowance	Adjusted basis
1	5.00	5.00	$5,000	$95,000
2	4.75	9.75	4,750	90,250
3	4.51	14.26	4,512	85,738
4	4.29	18.55	4,287	81,451
5	4.07	22.62	4,073	77,378
6	3.87	26.49	3,869	73,509
7	3.68	30.17	3,675	69,834
8	3.49	33.66	3,492	66,342
9	3.32	36.98	3,317	63,025
10	3.15	40.13	3,151	59,874
15	2.44	53.67	2,438	46,329
20	1.94	63.21	1,936	36,793
25	1.50	71.53	1,498	28,470
30	1.16	77.97	1,159	22,030
35	0.90	82.95	897	17,047
40	0.69	86.81	694	13,191

Index

Index